STOKELY WEBSTER

——

AND HIS PARIS

NEW YORK, LONDON

AND VENICE

STOKELY WEBSTER

———

AND HIS PARIS

NEW YORK, LONDON

AND VENICE

by STOKELY WEBSTER

LOWERY STOKES SIMS
Curator of Modern Art, The Metropolitan Museum of Art, New York

JOCK REYNOLDS
Director, Yale University Art Gallery

HAROLD C. SCHONBERG
American Critic, Former Student of Kuniyoshi, Cultural Correspondent of the New York Times

JON MONSON
Color Editor

LYNN MUELLER
Typography Editor

CONNECTICUT RIVER PRESS
HARTFORD

There is

a wonderful, distinctive charm in the work of

Stokely Webster, quality comprised of affection for the

world and a great understanding of light and value and

in the landscapes especially, a strong sense of place.

The paintings, so seemingly simple at first glance,

are each quiet revelations and a welcome confirmation

that continuity in art is not only possible in a harsh,

discordant time, but immensely gratifying.

What a joy it is to look at the life-work of a man

who knows exactly what he is about and

who so clearly loves life.

DAVID McCULLOUGH
Pulitzer Prize Historian

ACKNOWLEDGEMENTS

Full appreciation is due to the firms of Endo Graphics and Wolf ColorPrint for their backing of this publication. Their support is responsible for the scope of the presentation. More than one hundred and eighty original paintings were photographed with digital technology. Special thanks go to Silvia Victoria of Endo Graphics, Jeanne Wolf, Heather Habersang and Abe Shamasian of Wolf ColorPrint for their dedication and hard work.

Thanks are also due to all the museums that have allowed us to quote their publications and to print reproductions of Webster's work in their collections. These include, but are not limited to: The Metropolitan Museum of Art, New York; The Art Institute of Chicago; The Phillips Collection and The National Collection of American Art, both of Washington, DC; The High Museum, Atlanta, GA; The Albright-Knox Gallery, Buffalo, NY; The Indianapolis Museum of Art; The Denver Museum of Art; The Museum of Fine Arts, St. Petersburg, FL; The Elvehjem Museum, Madison, WI, and many others.

In the black and white photo sections, with the exception of the Peter Juley plates, page 40 and 52, all of the photographs were taken within the artist's immediate family and do not require credits.

Gracious permission to reproduce Webster's paintings in private collections was universally given where it was possible to contact the owner. Where contact could not be made, due to lost trails of provenance or other causes, the artist's right to reproduce his work is assumed since no exclusive rights to reproduce have ever been granted.

Printed in The United States of America

Connecticut River Press
91 Holmes Road
Newington, CT 06111
Phone (860) 666-0615
Fax (860) 594-0736

ISBN 0-9706573-0-7

Library of Congress Number 00-135141

CONTENTS

LUXEMBOURG GARDENS

1938

MY PARIS

"I can't say it in words, but I can say it in paint."

STOKELY WEBSTER

When I first saw Paris, I was just a few days past my tenth birthday. It was 1922 and Paris was still a walled city surrounded by earthen ramparts, with not much beyond except fields. It was the first city I had ever seen, except for a few glimpses of frightening, tall, windblown Chicago. The buildings in Paris were not more than six stories high. It was quiet, there were few cars. There was a beautiful river hugging the island at the exact center, where the city started growing more than a thousand years ago. On the island the cathedral of Notre Dame had been there for more than 800 years. This was heady stuff for a child who had lived, till then, in an area where the only historic monuments were Indian mounds.

I grew up in Paris! It was that year that I fell desperately in love with a girl twice my age. It was there that I first painted. It was in a suburb of Paris that I painted *St. Germain-en Lay* (Pl 1)and drew the *Chateau of Francis The First* (Pl 2).

I grew up in Paris and still think of it as a primary home. I go back to paint the river, the bridges and the broad boulevards. I marvel at its resilience, at its complete recovery from the tragedy of occupation. I marvel at the wisdom of the authorities in restricting skyscrapers to outside the walls, thus keeping the layout of Haussmann's radiating boulevards, and their intersections, with rond-points and their fountains, a thing of joy forever. That is my Paris. I can't say it in words, but I can say it in paint.

In some of the paintings, if you look for the motif today, you will find it changed. In *Under The Eifffel Tower*, painted in 1953 (Pl 6), the building in the background, The École Militaire is the same but behind it rises the skyscraper of The Gare de Montparnasse, which completely spoils the view. I would never paint this scene again as it looks today. It was this building that caused the Paris government to realize that it was a mistake and to cause them to ban nearly all future tall buildings near the center of the city. The new city of Paris with its daring modern buildings and skyscrapers is growing up beyond The Champs Élysées the Étoile and the Avenue de la Grande Armeé at La Défense. It also is beautiful but it is the old Paris that I love.

Another painting that you would find different today is *Avenue Des Invalides* (Pl 36). The change here is just that the dome of the Invalides has been covered with gold leaf. To paint this scene today the composition would have to be changed to conform with the new balance that shining gold creates.

The extraordinary thing however is how few of the motifs have changed. You can find most of them now, looking just the way I painted them many years ago. *The Place Furstenburg* painted in 1990 (Pl 7) still looks the same. It is on the left bank behind the church of St-Germain-des Prés. The door to the studio of Delacroix is at the very left edge of the painting. In *Metro la Tour Maubourg* 1970 (Pl 8), I remember that I was looking at the scene, not yet having made up my mind as to whether it was paintable or not, when a young workman rode up, chained his bike to the railing and descended into the Metro. The bike made the picture and I started painting at once.

I hope most of the paintings speak for themselves. The statue on the right in 'Facade, Notre Dame' (Pl 12) is of Charlemagne. There are two paintings of The Tuilleries Pond, both done in 1979 (Pls 14 and 39). In the distance you are looking up The Champs Élysées past the Obelisk on The Place de la Concord to, the Arc de Triomphe at The Étoile. The two boys in one of the paintings represent, in my mind myself and my younger brother, Roderick, for back in 1922 we spent hours sailing toy boats on this pond. The painting in (Pl 14) also has a story that in part explains my attachment to Paris. To paint this picture I had my easel/box set up on the very edge of the pond. I noticed that two gendarmes were coming along both sides making adults move their chairs back from the edge in order to give the children a better chance to sail their boats. I stayed put until one of them had almost reached me and then started to move my easel back. The gendarme called out to me not to move! "Vous être peintre, vous pouvez rester la!" You are a painter you may stay there! That says something! Most policemen in America would not show that deference to a painter.

Another motif that I painted more than once, was the Medici Fountain in The Luxembourg Gardens (Pls 24 and 25). I first saw this spot as a child of ten and the memory has stayed with me ever since. There is an interesting "trompe-l'oeil" effect, made by a 17th century architect that causes the still surface of the pond to appear to slope downhill. The Panthéon, with its great dome supported by a crown of columns was built by Louis XV and the architect, Soufflot. It is the burial place for many famous Frenchmen, Voltaire, Rousseau, Hugo and Zola to name just a few. As it dominates the skyline of the left bank, it appears in several of my paintings (Pls 29, 30, 32 and 33). The last two plates also show the pond in the Luxembourg Gardens, another place where we sailed toy boats. The building on the left in Pont Royal and the Louvre' (Pl 34) is the Pavillon de Flore of The Louvre and in the distance above the Pont Royal you can see Notre Dame on the Ile de la Cité. I think that there are few places in the world where in a short river excursion, one can see at close quarters so many and such beautiful historic buildings and landmarks!

ROMAN FRAGMENTS

1931

Pen and ink rendering on 30"x40" Watman paper—Beaux Arts Competition,
Yale School of Architecture

AN APPRECIATION

by

JOCK REYNOLDS

Director of Yale University Art Gallery

One of the joys of directing a university art gallery stems from the daily contact one has with the students, faculty, and alumni. One never tires of observing the effect that great art and inspirational teaching exert on the lives of young people, and it is always gratifying to hear accounts from returning alumni of what sometimes results from intense early encounters with art and learning. This monograph documenting the life and work of Stokely Webster tells the story of a man whose life changed course at Yale University, and traces the long trajectory of his artistic career as a painter.

For Stokely Webster, the years of 1931 and 1932 loomed large in his youth. His father, Henry Kitchell Webster, a successful author, knew his son loved art and possessed talent, but also fully understood the hazards of earning a living as a visual artist. After all, two of his good friends were the painters, Lawton Parker and Alson Clark. As the Great Depression tightened on America, the senior Webster directed young Stokely to attend the Yale School of Architecture. He enrolled his son in a professional course of study, wanting to see if he had the stamina and determination to develop his apparent abilities. The father surmised that a career in architecture might offer just the right blend of art and business that could afford his son a viable life in the creative arts.

Stokely was not unhappy with this arrangement, but at the school he chose to concentrate on the art side of his studies, where he found the "creative atmosphere" and many of his classmates inspiring. Eero Saarinen and Leslie Cheek were among the formidable students he met amidst endless hours studying free-hand drawing, drafting, and rendering. This basic training provided him with essential fundamental skills. The discipline required to complete Beaux Arts competitions on time "*en charette*" was also important to the young Webster. Above all, however, he found the inspiring lectures of Dean Everett Meeks to be the real blessing of Yale. It was Meeks' thoughtful and incisive words that helped inspire Stokely to pursue his burning desire to become a painter. And thus, rather than continue training as an architect, the young man left the School of Architecture before graduation, determined to follow his muse.

The account of Webster's early years as a painter is vividly described in the retrospective interview Lowery Stokes Sims has conducted with the now reflective senior artist. I commend it to your attention, for you will enjoy reading about how Stokely Webster proceeded to live the full and creative life he imagined for himself as a young man.

STUDY OF IVA, ON CHAIR

1931

The Metropolitan Museum of Art, New York

STOKELY WEBSTER

by

LOWERY STOKES SIMS

Curator of Modern Art, The Metropolitan Museum of Art, New York

June 1999

On the surface, Stokely Webster appears to lack the hallmarks of a modern-day painter. There is no "new way" to apply the paint, no innovative style, and some critics see in his work many derivative styles. This last observation may have merit. His first art instruction, at age ten, came from his honorary uncle, Lawton Parker, who had been a pupil of Whistler, Carolus Duran and Gérôme. Parker taught what he had been taught and he also had young Webster studying the draftsmanship of Raphael, Michelangelo and Degas. Later, Webster largely taught himself to paint by studying and sometimes copying paintings in the Metropolitan Museum. He says that for any painting he really liked, he wanted to learn the technique that had made it possible.

Thus he developed a strong and very versatile technique. Carlyle Burrows noted, as early as 1940, that Webster's oil paintings reminded one of Sargent's brilliance. As to the criticism that he displayed no one unique style, Henry McBride pointed out nearly sixty years ago that "His manner of painting changes with the subject. The subject seems to move him to choose a technique that is particularly suited to that subject. He has a natural way of expressing himself and he shuns routine."

He shunned routine because to him painting was a joy, and except for short periods, not a "food on the table" job. That side of life was taken care of by his work as an engineer. He worked as an engineer and executive with the Grumman Corporation, building fighter planes for the Navy. Because of this he was able to paint the way he had been taught to paint as a boy and to paint because he loved it!

He loved it because it enabled him to save for future viewing and for others, those especial beauties of nature and man's wonderful additions to nature that he found so tantalizingly satisfying. His paintings may have nothing new with which to create another "ism" but they are something else important; they are an honest portrayal of an artist's view of the world. Indubitably he is an important artist.

I was recently pleased to visit the artist in his Connecticut studio, to talk to him about being interviewed for this book.

When asked, his response was positive and enthusiastic. He said, "I hate to write but I love to talk." He liked the idea of the book. He thought it would give his children—his paintings—"more light of day!" He also said that he has many memories of events that happened 70 or 80 years ago,that led him to be a painter. These might be of interest to young people today who are thinking of traditional painting as a career.

Stokely Webster and his paintings have very recently experienced a true renaissance. Fifty-nine years ago, before WWII, all the major New York art critics acclaimed his paintings, and forecast for him "a sure success."

SAINT GERMAIN-EN-LAYE

1938

The Phillips Collection, Washington, D.C.

It didn't happen right away! The war came and went and a new group of critics took over the major newspapers, and his paintings were no longer considered the "in thing." As he tells it, he was either too stubborn or too sure that his paintings were good the way they were, to be willing to change his style to keep up with the times.

For forty years Webster's friends knew him as an engineer. His painting career was pushed aside, to weekends and evenings, so that he could continue to paint as he wished, without financial consequences. Engineering kept food on the table and a roof overhead, while he continued to paint, as he says, "As I damn well pleased." More than a decade ago, he retired with a pension from engineering, and returned full-time to painting, but still in no rush to bring the paintings to market. It was still too soon for important galleries to see this work as something "cool." That has now dramatically changed and Webster says he definitely believes that life begins at eighty!

Webster, now at the age of eighty-seven, lives with his wife, Audrey, in a lovely home on the Connecticut shore, in semi-retirement. These interviews took place at his home and here in New York. Some of the information on family history which follows is taken from a small book that Stokely's father, Henry Kitchell Webster, wrote in memory of his father, Towner Keeney Webster, shortly after the latter's death in 1922.

INTERVIEW — EARLY YEARS

You've said that you see yourself as bridging the gap between the 19th and 21th centuries. What do you think your work and artistic philosophy mean for the future?

My hope is that it might reawaken, in at least a part of the art world, an appreciation of values once considered basic to the art of painting. Things like draftsmanship, composition, harmony and beauty, which have, ever since World War II, to a great extent been replaced by "newness" for newness' sake.

As for what I said about bridging a century gap, my first teacher, in 1922, was Lawton Parker. He had studied in the 1890s at the Beaux Arts and with Whistler, Gérôme, and Carolus Duran. He instilled in me techniques and values that were in fact basic to the art of the past and were taken for granted by most of the art world up until shortly before World War II. Not many people are aware of them now, so I see the possibility of being able to relate them even, God willing, into the coming century to anyone who might want to listen. That is what I meant by a bridge. As I said, my artistic philosophy is embodied in my paintings. It speaks of composition, harmony, and elements that I do not think will hurt the future.

I think that's obvious! Now, let's start from the beginning. Tell us about your early life.

I was born in Evanston, Illinois, just before the First World War. I remember saving peach pits for gas masks. My father, Henry Kitchell Webster, was an author and had already published several novels before I was born. My mother was a beautiful lady. She had graduated with the first class at Northwestern University that accepted women. Our house, at 1411 Maple Avenue, Evanston, was large and square. My father's father and mother lived in the house next door. Close by, and in the adjacent village of Winnetka, lived all six of their children and many grandchildren. It was a close family; Thanksgiving and Christmas festivities were family gatherings that stretched the capacity of their house.

I want to tell you about Grandfather. Let's use the little book my father wrote about him to get the facts straight. His name was Towner Keeney Webster, born in Ithaca, NY. By the time I knew him he had become an important Chicago industrialist and entrepreneur. He had started The Webster Manufacturing Co. and The Webster Electric Co., both successful. He also had misadventures, like backing and building a factory to produce "The Page Compositor," an amazing typesetting machine that predated the Mergenthaler Linotype by several years. It was too complicated to be practical and was later completely replaced by the Linotype before it ever got into production. Samuel Clemens (Mark Twain) also lost money in this venture. The family had good years and bad. Towner's wife, Emma Josephine, used to say she didn't know whether they would be taking a trip to Europe, or whether she would

TOWNER KEENEY WEBSTER and EMMA JOSEPHINE KITCHELL

HENRY KITCHELL WEBSTER Jr., TOWNER KEENEY WEBSTER AND
HENRY KITCHELL WEBSTER

have to choose which color spool of thread to buy, because she couldn't afford to buy two.

Emma Josephine's parents, Silas and Frances Kitchell, were living in Chicago at the time of the Great Fire of 1871. They were burnt out and had to flee by wagon and on foot, with what possessions they could carry, along the lakefront to Evanston, twelve miles to the north.

Towner had come West in 1866 to make his start in Chicago. Soon after, his widowed mother sold her home in Ithaca, NY, and moved her household goods via the Erie Canal and Great Lakes Steamer to Chicago and then to Evanston. Towner and Emma Josephine met at the Baptist Church in Evanston. They were married in 1874.

WHEN WAS YOUR FATHER BORN? WHAT WAS HIS POSITION IN THE FAMILY?

My father was born in 1875. He was the eldest of six children. One of his chores as a child was driving the family cow from the barn behind their house to the pasture, west of town. He graduated from Hamilton College in 1897 and taught English Literature at Union College the next year.

WHAT ABOUT YOUR MOTHER?

My mother, Mary Ward Orth, was born in Hiawatha, Kansas. Her grandparents and great-grandparents were whalers living in New Bedford, Massachusetts. They were descendants of John and Priscilla Alden. My mother and father were married in 1901. They had three children, all boys. Henry Kitchell Jr. was born in 1905, I was born in 1912, and Roderick Sheldon in 1915.

WHAT ARE YOUR EARLIEST MEMORIES?

My earliest consecutive memories are of the farm. It was a real farm, one hundred miles west of Chicago, on the Rock River, four miles north of Oregon, Illinois. There were about a hundred and fifty acres of corn and wheat fields, stretching along the river. On the far side of the fields, a steep wooded hill climbed about sixty feet above the flood plain and then descended again into a meadow and pasture with a creek. There were the farmhouses, barns and silos. There were horses, cows, chickens and hogs wallowing in the mud. It was an unusual place for my grandfather to own, for he was an industrialist, not a farmer. The story that he gave his six children regarding this purchase was that he wanted a place where he could alienate his grandchildren's affection from their parents. It is evident that he loved to tease.

My grandfather took an immediate liking to Henry Tice, the farmer from whom he had purchased the land. He made a deal that allowed Tice to go on farming the arable part of the property and retain the income from it, while he had some of the wooded area cleared where he built a large summer residence.

His son, my uncle Maurice, graduated from Cornell Architecture School in the spring of 1917 and his first job was designing and supervising the construction of this residence. The great room for both living and dining had a cathedral ceiling and an immense chimney and fireplace, which a child could walk into. It was built with great stones from a quarry across the creek. I remember these stones being blasted out of the quarry and dragged by horse teams to the building site. Horses pulling bucket scoops were used to excavate for the swimming pool. More woods were cleared and small cottages were built by several of my uncles and aunts. My father had one built of cedar that could sleep up to eight people. It had three rooms and a large screened-in porch.

By mid-summer of 1918, Bee Tree Farm was ready for opening ceremonies and Grandfather invited more than three hundred guests, from surrounding farms and from Chicago to a mammoth clam bake. Two pits were dug, each six-by-eight feet and about six feet deep. The day of the party, a refrigerated freight car was delivered to the Oregon siding with bushels of clams and wet seaweed. The bottoms of the pits were filled with burning logs and charcoal, then layers of cheesecloth sacks of clams, chickens, yams, ears of corn and pearl onions. These were topped by more seaweed and left to cook for hours. I remember long lines of plank tables and benches set out on the lawn, and next to the cider press a mountain of apples, towering over my head.

STOKELY, HIS MOTHER (IN LIGHT SUIT) AND RODERICK,
ON THE *REGINA* ON THE WAY TO ENGLAND, 1922

For the next fifteen years, this magical place was my summer domain. I am sure it had an influence on my view of the world and hence on my future paintings.

WHAT WAS IT EXACTLY THAT INFLUENCED THE CHARACTER OF YOUR PAINTING?

I think it was the beauty of the place, combined with the luxury of having free time to absorb it and revel in it. It was a "raison d'être" in itself. I feel that it encompassed a feeling of contentment which, if it could be captured in a painting, might impart to a viewer a bit of that contentment and "joie de vivre." It didn't occur to me at that young age that such a painting could be possible. However, at age ten when I first saw Monet's paintings, I suddenly thought maybe it was possible—and that changed my life.

TELL US MORE ABOUT THE FARM.

The summers here were a large family affair. My cousins and their mothers would eat their meals with their grandparents at the big house, which made a goodly number at the table. On weekends, when the fathers and their guests arrived, there could be as many as thirty and extra tables had to be set up for the children.

This operation continued little changed after my grandfather died in 1922. My grandmother, affectionately called Aunt Jo, took over the supervision of the clan, with the willing help of all six of her children. A woman named Mrs. Grush was paid to come in to help in the kitchen. She weighed well over 200 pounds and was very jolly.

With the working part of the farm just a half mile down the road, a great deal of the food for the table came from there. I remember searching the haylofts for eggs and, with the help of a couple of cousins, rounding up chickens to bring back to Mrs. Grush, who was very good with an ax. There were corn, tomatoes and all kinds of vegetables to be picked in the gardens and there were berries from the hedgerows.

I will never forget the pleasure of wandering by the creek and drinking in the beauty of the whole effect of the willows against the blue of the sky and the great floating clouds.

But I didn't spend all my time in contemplation, I also helped (or hindered) Mr. Tice and his fellow farmers in feeding the hogs and gathering in the hay and oats. The climax was harvest week, starting with the arrival of the community threshing machine and the great self propelled steam engine that ran it. The threshing machine and the great flywheel of the steam engine were connected by a wide sixty-foot-long belt. The scene was one of sweltering heat, the blazing sun, the smell of freshcut hay, the clanking of the thresher, the hissing of steam, the flapping of the great belt and the shouting of orders to the teams pulling the wagons.

PORTRAIT OF STOKELY'S MOTHER BY LAWTON PARKER
PARIS, 1904

STOKELY AT THE FARM, 1920

STOKELY AND HIS FATHER, 1917

YOU HAVE A PHOTOGRAPH HERE OF YOURSELF AT THE FARM IN 1920.

Yes. I would like to tell you something about this child. He has been, and is in a way, my role model. I try to maintain what I can of his view of the world. I remember and I can still see in my eyes in that photo, a world of expectant fulfillment, of limitless attainable horizons and a certain inner relaxed confidence. It isn't an easy thing to retain, I admit! One has to face up to the facts. But, to the extent possible, hanging on to that expectant view of the future enhances the chance of achieving it.

WHAT GAVE YOU THAT FEELING OF EXPECTANCY, OF LIMITLESS POSSIBILITIES? WHAT GAVE YOU THAT SENSE OF CONFIDENCE?

Well, remember we are talking about me as a child. I don't necessarily maintain that confidence today. I just try to. You can say that it was in his nature and certainly my parents and grandparents reveal some of the same tendencies, but I feel that the time and place of my birth are also crucial. The early years of the twentieth century were exciting times to be young in America's Midwest. It is hard to believe now, but I remember that among my parents' generation and sometimes with my peers, there was an imbued sense of pride in being so closely related to those amazing Americans who set this country up as an independent nation. Those men, the Tom Paines, the Washingtons, the Jeffersons and the Minute Men, defeated one of the greatest armies on earth and

STOKELY, ON HIS FIRST BIRTHDAY

S.W. AT ABOUT FOUR

went on to produce a Declaration of Independence and a Constitution that inaugurated a form of government never before seen in the history of the world. It allowed a completely unprecedented degree of individual freedom.

People in the Chicago area at the turn of the century were keenly aware of the benefits of this freedom. They did not forget that it was won in the very recent past by their own forebears. The fruits of this hard-won freedom were everywhere to be seen and marveled at. My grandfather witnessed the building of the first railroad to cross the continent and he enjoyed recounting his adventures. You know, had I been able to live my 86 years in reverse, from 1912, I would have come within one year of being able to speak to Thomas Jefferson and John Adams in person.

WHAT WAS THE MIDWEST LIKE AT THAT TIME? YOUR FAMILY WAS INSTRUMENTAL IN THE DEVELOPMENT OF CHICAGO, WEREN'T THEY?

In a way, yes. Chicago was a hub and the railroads and Great Lakes steamers hauled great quantities of grain that were transferred and stored in mammoth grain elevators. It was The Webster Manufacturing Co., started by my grandfather, that built these elevators and the machinery that ran them. Two of my father's first novels, "Short Line War" and "Calumet K," were about the romance of building a short railroad and a grain elevator. The excitement and exuberance of the times were very close to home and made ambitious dreams seem normal.

THE OTHER PLACE WHERE YOU SPENT YOUR YOUTH WAS EVANSTON, ILLINOIS. WHAT DO YOU REMEMBER ABOUT YOUR LIFE THERE?

I lived at 1411 Maple Ave., Evanston, until I was nineteen. It brings back countless pleasant recollections. It was a large wooden house built in the 1870's. It is still there, preserved as an historic landmark for its architecture.

STOKELY WEBSTER, AGE NINE, IN A BOAT
ON THE RIVER WYE IN WALES

The rooms had twelve-foot ceilings and the living room was almost forty feet long. It had tall windows facing west that let in floods of afternoon sunshine. I remember the house as taking on the warmth of personality that my parents imbued it with.

How were their personalities expressed in the house?

My mother was a warm and gracious woman, with a great sense of artistic balance and beauty. She had furnished the house with a happy mixture of comfortable contemporary sofas and Victorian masterpieces, all on a limited budget. She picked out the materials for the drapes and sewed them herself. Indirect lighting was almost unheard of at that time (there were still gas fixtures in part of the house) but mother got bright electric bulbs for the living room ceiling and hid them behind grass warriors' shields from Borneo. There were other trophies decorating the room that my parents had acquired on their round-the-world trip in 1910. There was a batik from Java on the grand piano, a Foo Dog from Singapore, brass trays from India and Oriental rugs from Persia.

You mentioned that your father was a novelist. Did he make a living from his writing?

He did. By the time I was seven, he had become a well-known author in the Chicago area. Fifteen of his novels had been published, several of them best sellers, and many were serialized in The Saturday Evening Post before they appeared in hard back. One of our great pleasures was to listen to my father read to mother, my brothers and me what he had written that week. He took our comments seriously, even my seven-year-old views, or so I believed. His own writing was but a small part of what he read to us. He loved the sound of the English language and would read out loud by the hour, even if only one of us was listening, authors like Jane Austen, Dickens, Galsworthy, and Winston Churchill. They were warm, cozy family evenings, sometimes making it hard to pull away to get homework done.

Where did you go to school?

I went to North Shore Country Day, in the close-by village of Winnetka. I went there from kindergarten through twelfth grade. I was most fortunate. It was a private school, at the time considered progressive, but that term means something very different today. Then, it was progressive to teach the history of Western civilization in context with geography, art and the biographies of the major protagonists. History was tied in with the literature of English and other language courses, it was not just a matter of memorizing dates and wars.

WHEN YOU WERE STILL RELATIVELY YOUNG, NINE YEARS OLD IN FACT, YOUR FAMILY SPENT A YEAR AND A HALF IN EUROPE. THAT MUST HAVE BEEN AN EXCITING TIME FOR YOU.

It was! I skipped the fifth grade at North Shore, for that was the year the family spent in Europe. The adventure started in the early spring of 1922 when I was nine. I was not sure of all of the reasons for the trip, but I do feel that a major one was the enhancement of our education. My parents had visited many lands before I was born and were certainly aware of the benefits of travel.

I feel that for me, it was certainly a great blessing! Already entranced by the wonders and beauty of the outdoors, I now discovered that man's hand, as applied by architects, sculptors, landscapers, bridge builders and gardeners, could make the "en plein air" even more inspiring. I could not get enough of it and wandered around, wide-eyed, especially in Paris. I marveled at the richness of the ambiance and the sidewalk cafés with crowds of people enjoying life. The tree-lined broad avenues, with "rond points" and statues and fountains, and behind it all fascinating history. The year and a half went by much too fast!

NOWADAYS WE SIMPLY GET ON A PLANE AND FLY TO EUROPE. HOW DID YOU MAKE THE JOURNEY IN 1922?

The trip started by train, from Chicago to Rochester, then by lake steamer to the head of the Saint Lawrence River. We then took a smaller boat, shooting the Lachine Rapids and on down to Montreal. There we boarded the White Star liner Regina for Liverpool, England.

We spent much of the summer in England, among other things, seeking out the inns Mr. Pickwick had visited to check on Dickens' descriptions. By fall we were in Paris, where we rented an apartment at 12 Rue Perignon, near the Place de Breteuil and the Place des Invalides. I saw the exhibition of Impressionist painters at the Luxembourg Palace and it changed my life!

HOW DID IT CHANGE YOUR LIFE?

I had already visited The Louvre with my mother and seen the classic landscapes of Poussin, Lorraine, Fragonard and Watteau, without being too excited. But these Monets and Sisleys were something altogether different. They were, for me, "real." They actually captured the same beautiful feeling about "nature" that I was used to enjoying when out in the open air, in the streets of Paris or the pasture at the farm. It came as a kind of shock to discover that this feeling could be captured in paint. Then and there, I made up my mind that I was going to be a painter!

WITH WHOM DID YOU STUDY ART?

With Lawton Parker. My mother and father had gotten to know him twelve years before this, in Paris. He was an American painter who had roots in Chicago, having been the head of instruction at the Chicago Art Institute and at his own Parker Academy. The Websters and Lawton Parker became such good friends that in later years we children were encouraged to call him "Uncle Lawton." He had a studio in Paris on the Boulevard Kellerman. When I made up my mind to be a painter, it was natural to go to Uncle Lawton for help. His studio and lifestyle did nothing but intensify my determination to paint. As I mentioned before, Lawton Parker had studied at the École des Beaux Arts, the Academie Julien and the Academie Carmen, with Gérôme, Carolus Duran and Whistler. I was pleased that Parker agreed to give me lessons. I learned how to mix paint bravely, how to see perspective and the great importance of drawing. He had me copying Old Master drawings, with insight into the Masters' use of lines, where to start a line and where to stop it, how to gain an almost magical three-dimensional effect by hanging onto the thought of solidity with every line. Finally, I received the advice I wanted most, "Go out in the street and paint!"

I bought a paint box that I could hold on my lap or place on a café table. One of the first paintings I did, was of the facade of Notre Dame as seen from a Left Bank café on the Quai St. Michel. Another was painted in the park at Saint Germain-en-Laye and several were of the Luxembourg Gardens. Only the Park in St. Germain remains. The rest were destroyed in a studio fire, in 1952.

Uncle Lawton suggested that we make the trip to Giverny, where Monet was still painting. Lawton had spent many summers there, at one time sharing a studio with Guy Rose. My mother and I made the trip by train. Although I did not get a picture painted, I did get a glimpse of Monet, at work in his garden.

THE CATHeDRAL

FOUR DRAWINGS FROM
THE 1922 NOTEBOOK—AGE TEN
THE ART INSTITUTE OF CHICAGO

LANGEAIS

26

There were other trips out from Paris, besides the one to Giverny. They went to Chartres, Senlis, Soissons, the coast of Brittany and the Chateaux of the Loire. On these trips, Stokely kept a little notebook in which he made sketches and a few notes about the places they saw. It is interesting to take note of the difference in his proficiency in writing and in drawing.

When the school year started, Kitchell enrolled at the Sorbonne and Stokely and Roderick went to school at The Academy Cazin in Lausanne, Switzerland and later to school at St. Germain-En-Laye.

In addition to the little notebook diary that Stokely kept himself, there was a more extensive, off-and-on diary, kept by his father, of his dictated account of the day's activities. Stokely does not know why it was "his" words that were written down, unless it was that his father had in mind a novel in which a ten-year-old boy played a major role and he wanted to observe how they talk. In any case he wrote down Stokely's exact words, verbatim. In some places these words seem to indicate almost as clearly as do the drawings, the youngster's preoccupation with the visual aspect of things, as in this account of a boat trip from Geneva to Lausanne.

"We caught one glimpse of Mont Blanc before we took the boat. It was a rainy day, but that made the trip all the prettier, because the sun came out a little and made rainbows. We counted six and one of them was unusually bright. We could see the sides of the mountain and little villages right through it. It made them look all different colors. The storm clouds hanging around the snow-capped mountains, with crimson edges and the sun shining on them, were very pretty indeed. On the way back on the boat a flock of gulls followed us. When we threw bread in the air they would catch it. Lausanne was very pretty at night, all lighted up, as we approached on the boat."

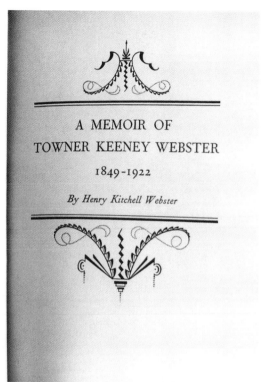

A MEMOIR OF
TOWNER KEENEY WEBSTER
1849-1922

By Henry Kitchell Webster

THE HOUSE IN EVANSTON
1411 MAPLE AVE.

PORCH OF THE BIG HOUSE AT THE FARM

THE GOLIATH

WERE YOU ENROLLED IN SCHOOL IN PARIS DURING YOUR YEAR ABROAD?

Rod and I were at the Academy Cazin in Switzerland. It was on the hill that rises from the port of Ouchy to Lausanne. There is an inclined railway and the school was near the mid-way stop. Rod and I were to spend the winter there, except for Christmas vacation, when we would return to the apartment in Paris.

My chief recollections of the school are of its beautiful surroundings, the terraced gardens, the view of Lac Lemon and the snow-capped mountains beyond it, the fragrance of the boxwood and the clear crisp air. I also remember playing "football" (really soccer) in shorts, in the snow, of trying to speak and think in French, as no one would speak to me in English. There were meals of bread and enormous terrines of thick, hot, homemade soup. There were the Sunday parades of all the boys in uniform, along the Quai at Ouchy and the footpath along the lake. I remember, most of all, falling hopelessly in love with the headmaster's daughter, twice my age and with whom I had spoken only a few words. I vowed, by the light of a brilliant moon, to return someday to marry her!

Back in Paris at Christmas, Mother had a treat for us. She had booked passage on the first Trans-Channel commercial air flight, Paris to London. It had only been thirteen years since Louis Blériot had his historic first flight across the Channel, so this was definitely an adventure! The plane was a converted German World War I bomber, named The Goliath. The conversion was minimal. The passenger compartment was the bomb bay with a wooden floor covering the bomb bay doors. Tiny windows had been cut in the side walls and wicker lawn furniture installed. As I remember it, there was room for about eight passengers. The flight was overbooked, so a second plane was added. This second plane never made it to London but was forced down on the British coast with mechanical trouble. The first section, that we were in, made it to Croydon, at that time the Aerodrome for London. We boys were very pleased with the adventure!

WHAT DID YOU DO WHEN THE YEAR WAS UP?

We gave up the Paris apartment and picked up on the "Grand Tour" of the previous summer. More of France, Bordeaux, Provence, and the Riviera. Then Spain, Madrid, Toledo and El Greco's house, the Alhambra, and Barcelona. We saw Italy with the Leaning Tower, the palaces of Venice, the Blue Grotto, and finally, on to Sicily.

It was one unbelievable sight after another! Mont St. Michel, the fishing villages of Brittany, the caves at Lascaux, the Basque Country, the blazing sun and deep shade of Aix-en-Provence and The Cours Mirabeau. Venice was a completely unforgettable mirage of a city floating in the sea. I have been back there countless times, but can never get enough of it. I revisit all these places, both in fact and in memory, reliving those glorious experiences of childhood.

Finally we sailed from Palermo to New York, back to Evanston and reality! With our return to the States, I

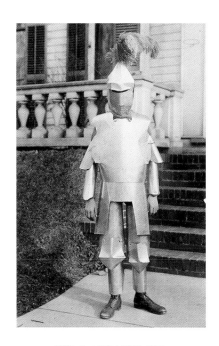

SIR LAUNCELOT

was brought back to a comparatively humdrum existence of school and homework.

WHAT WAS IT ABOUT SCHOOL THAT YOU DIDN'T LIKE AFTER SUCH AN EXCITING YEAR?

It wasn't that I didn't like school. I always did like most of my classes, but there was one that was a little hard to take. That was the art class. The fifth and sixth grade art instructor had an art show of his students' summer work. I, of course, had not been there the winter before, had nonetheless done summer artwork and submitted several of my recent paintings. I was much upset when the teacher, in front of the class, rejected my work on the basis that it was obviously not the work of a ten-year-old. He went on to say that he didn't like cheating! I did not honor him by responding. Of course I failed art that year!

The art class, however, was the only class that was not rewarding. For the most part, I was eager to learn and did well in school. There was a study hall with a good library, where high-school students could do their homework in class breaks. There, I found The Comptons Pictured Encyclopedia and spent many hours engrossed in it. I learned how a four-cycle gasoline engine works, how airplanes fly and other equally important matters, somewhat at the expense of my proficiency in Latin.

WHAT ELSE DID YOU LIKE ABOUT SCHOOL?

I participated enthusiastically in the plays and operettas that the upper-class students put on each year. Once I sang the part of the Mikado in Gilbert and Sullivan's light opera of that name. I think I acquitted myself quite well, especially in the deep guttural laughs, for I was inspired by my father's joyous rendition of many of the Gilbert and Sullivan pattersongs on the living room Steinway. I also played the part of Tom, the penniless playwright, in Arthur Pinero's comedy "Tralawney of the Wells." I remember that after Dad saw one of the performances of this play, he said to me, "If you wanted to be an actor you would probably do very well." I took this as a sincere compliment, for my father was not in the habit of saying things he did not mean. He knew a lot about the theater. He had many friends who were successful actors or opera stars. He had written a play "June Madness," and attended it's Broadway rehearsals, with Ethel Barrymore as the star.

I REMEMBER YOU TELLING ME ABOUT YOUR CAVE PROJECT. WILL YOU TALK ABOUT THAT?

My summers at the farm continued to be the best part of the year for me. As I remember it, I was a somewhat aloof child. I had several cousins about my age, with whom I could have played had I wanted to, but I usually preferred my own thoughts. For me there was always something interesting to do. With no suggestion or encouragement from anyone else, I embarked on this cave project. I feel as though I paid my tribute to several art forms before they were invented and before I was fourteen!

This must have started with a basic instinct to tunnel. I first got the whole scheme figured out in my mind and then started to dig straight into the side of the hill next to the big house. It was easy digging, for in that part of Illinois, the top soil is very thick. The tunnel was just big enough to crawl into, on hands and knees. It started straight, but very soon began to turn and kept on turning until, about 15 feet from where it started, it broke out above ground again. From there I dug a trench, some 25 feet to the bottom of the hill, and covered it over with boards, just below the ground line. I finished off with four inches of dirt and grass seed, to completely conceal it. At the low end of this fake tunnel, I dug a pit the size of a small room and deep enough to stand up in. It, too, was covered over with boards and concealed with a thin layer of dirt and grass.

Now came the important testing! The reaction from other children who had witnessed none of the construction was just what I had hoped it would be. The creation was not just a "Trompe l'oeil," but a "Trompe Direction Sense" as well. People crawling into the cave lost their orientation as soon as they were in the dark and, failing to realize that they had made a complete "U" turn, thought that they were descending deep into the earth. With my strong claustrophobic fears, I would never have been able to make the passage to the underground room, had I not known what my peers didn't know, that it was only four inches underground, not the 30 feet it appeared to be. One could have escaped at any time by just pushing on the ceiling. I believe that no adult ever entered into this room of treasures.

So, how did you further pursue this inventive inclination?

Well, I created an electric automobile, a true triumph for early "Performance Art." Up until 1920, there were no public utilities at the farm. Water was pumped by windmill and what dim electricity there was, was supplied by a twelve-volt gasoline-driven Delco generator and stored in green glass, lead acid batteries. When the power lines were finally extended north from Oregon, this twelve-volt equipment became obsolete, including a twelve-volt motor that had pumped water when the wind failed.

Also obsolete was a beautiful carriage that had once been pulled by a team of ponies. The urge to make use of "found objects" was irresistible. I screwed 48 angle irons to the spokes of a rear wheel of the carriage and mounted the motor with a pulley on its shaft directly above, providing belt power to the circle of angle irons. The shaft the ponies had pulled on was sawed and hinged back into the vehicle, making a fine tiller for steering. The glass batteries were mounted in the rear seat and connected to the motor with a switch.

The moment of "performance" had arrived! In view of a curious family crowd and a 16 mm movie camera, the vehicle descended the steep driveway at great speed, with me at the tiller and no brakes! It continued on the full length of a half mile of new test strip of concrete pavement. However, my electric buggy was unable to remount the driveway and having fulfilled its destiny was soon re-relegated to the category of obsolete parts.

Webster talks of many more projects some big, some small, like the suit of armor he made for himself out of tin, to play the part of Launcelot in a Christmas pageant written by his father. He cut the patterns and then cut and riveted the tin to fit his size. Actually the armor came first and his father wrote the pageant piece to make use of it.

It was about this time that you met Iva, whom you would later marry!

Yes, summers at the farm became even more interesting with the arrival of Iva, my cousin by adoption. She was a little older than I, but had a more difficult childhood, with little chance to enjoy such pleasures as swimming and tennis. I was able to introduce her to many such pleasures. We were doing everything together, driving in to Oregon for a black and white soda, diving in the pool, lying in the sun and best of all, spending hours on the river at night in the canoe.

Yes, we fell in love. The river was wide and slow moving. At night the sky was brilliant with stars and the complete darkness of the river made the water look black. The banks, with their low hills, were only barely visible. The silence was so complete that all you could hear was the dip and swish of the paddle. We would let the canoe drift and lie together in the bottom, watching the sky patterns move to the west, and talk softly of dreams, which as the weeks went by became more plans than dreams. There were gentle kisses, but nothing more.

Discussions of sex with one's father were very uncommon, for the Victorian taboos were still in effect. I remember that my father said he felt that it was important not to experience too many of life's gratifications too early, before their significance could be fully appreciated. He added, "You miss all the pleasures of anticipation."

We enjoyed the pleasures of anticipation for a few more years! We were married on my twenty-first birthday, in 1933.

You mentioned that Iva was your "adopted" cousin. Would you explain that?

Iva was the adopted child of Walter Kitchell, my grandmother's youngest brother. She had been born in 1908 to Hugh and Emma Baugh, in Junction City, Kansas, and given her mother's name. She became an orphan at the age of three by the death of her mother of tuberculosis and the disappearance of her father. She remained in an orphanage about a year and was then adopted by 52- year-old Robert Walter Kitchell and his much younger wife Ora. Ora was definitely the stage mother type and apparently planned from the start that this cute child would be a stage celebrity!

Emma's name was changed to Iva. Her curly hair was dyed blond, and she was continuously embarrassed by her new mother's frequent remark to friends that her child was going to be a movie star. Walter Kitchell may have been too old and too unfamiliar with civilian life to care. He had spent much of his bachelor's life as a non-commissioned officer in the Spanish American War.

When Iva was eight, her new father fell into debt, gambling. He forged a signature on a check to pay the obligation. His fellow officer, whose name he forged, reported him. He was court martialed and spent some time in prison. In order to raise the train fare to get herself and her mother to her aunt's home in Michigan, Iva had to give a dance performance. Ora resumed the occupation she had before her marriage, making hats and sewing fur. Iva earned money selling produce from a neighbor's farm and winning "amateur night" contests on weekends.

When Walter was released from prison, his spirits were so crushed that he was unable to get or keep a job. For a while Ora operated a boardinghouse, Iva did the cooking, washing and ironing. Her mother induced boarders to come and her fastidious father, sometimes drove them away by making remarks about their table manners.

Iva was torn in her allegiance. She loved her father's refined use of language and his great knowledge of good literature, but she also realized that it was her mother who kept food on the table.

When Iva was almost fourteen her mother got her to audition for a place in a vaudeville act. She passed the test and was promised a salary for fifteen weeks. Her mother saw this as the opportunity she had so long sought. She got herself a job as wardrobe mistress with the company. They gave up the boardinghouse and set off to conquer the world on Iva's shoulders. The expectations did not last long!

The very first week on tour in Grand Rapids, Michigan, the show was stopped by the Gary Society, on the grounds that it employed underage children. The manager was fined and the act disbanded. At long last Walter was forced to do, what he had so long avoided, that is seek help from his sister, my grandmother. The little family of three descended on her doorstep, unannounced, seeking shelter.

My grandfather had recently passed away, and my grandmother was able to take them in to live with her. They accepted, but at the same time felt an obligation to be useful. They did this by taking over many of the household chores. Again Iva did ironing and lots of baby-sitting for several Webster families in the neighborhood.

Our house was next door to Grandmother's and I could not help but notice the industrious, bashful child with the blond curls. I felt that she was not being treated as her other cousins were, with a chance to spend time playing at the farm.

Her mother held her in tight rein and continued to try to get her into a vaudeville act. Every time she could get away from her sewing duties, she would rush little Iva into Chicago to audition for one act or another. I wondered why none of the family intervened on the child's behalf. It seemed that no one wanted to argue with her mother who still felt that Iva was her future road to wealth and luxury.

DID IVA FINALLY HAVE ANY SUCCESS WITH HER PERFORMING?

Yes, definitely! There was one Webster, Maurice the architect, who apparently saw the same remarkable qualities in Iva that I did. Uncle Maurice, or Mouse as everyone called him, had long talks with her and sensing her talent and genuine desire to succeed in the theatre, he offered to pay for her to study at the prestigious Pavley-Oukrainsky Ballet School in Chicago.

TELL US ABOUT THAT SCHOOL. WAS IT A MODERN DANCE SCHOOL? A BALLET SCHOOL?

Pavley and Oukrainsky had been partners of Pavlova on her recent world tour. They had capitalized on this publicity to obtain the directorship of the Chicago Opera Company Ballet and had also set up a ballet school in Chicago. Iva accepted Maurice's offer and took the El into Chicago to register at the school. She inquired of the registrar how long it would take to get into the company. The response from Edris Millar, who later became a good friend, was, "My dear, most pupils never make it and the least time would be several years!" Iva signed up and worked and practiced so hard that within seven months she was accepted into the company. Almost immediately she was doing bit solo character parts, something for which she had an instinctive aptitude. Several years later, Massine, director of the Ballet Russe De Monte Carlo, offered her a part in the road company. He explained that she could not be in the New York company, because there, his wife did the parts Iva was being considered for.

Iva had an innate facility with satire and comedy of the extremely subtle kind. She loved the ballet when it was top-notch, but she was amused by and liked to kid the ballerina who held an arabesque too long, or took exaggerated preparation for a difficult feat. Iva had developed such a strong technique and she could do the things she was satirizing so well, that the point was made with refinement and the audience loved it.

She worked out a program and was able to give a whole evening's solo concert complete with twelve or fourteen numbers. With the assistance of a pianist and the management of Sol Hurok and the National Concert and Artists Corporation, she gave over a thousand concerts all over the world. She had sold out performances at Carnegie Hall, one of them with the New York Philharmonic, at the main opera houses of Buenos Aires, Rio de Janeiro, and Bogota. She had a Presidential command performance at the opera house in Montevideo. (There is a review of one of her programs by Paul Hume on page 368.)

WHAT WAS HAPPENING WITH REGARD TO YOUR PAINTING AT THIS TIME?

After our return from Europe, my painting career had a lapse of almost six years. There was simply too much to do, to get through high school and prepare for college to find the time and energy to paint. Also I was seduced by another fascinating pursuit, flying.

In those days in Illinois, a driver's license did not exist; one could drive at any age. One day when I was fourteen, I was driving on a country road west of Evanston, when I came upon an amazing sight! A World War I biplane parked in a field beside the road and a sign, hanging on the fence, saying: FLYING LESSONS $5. I must have had some kind of intuition about this, because for some time I had been saving my allowance. I had five dollars in my pocket and more at home in the kitty. Naturally I took advantage of this unique opportunity!

The barnstorming pilot was also of World War I vintage and wore a purple scarf and goggles. The plane was a Curtiss Jenny, with an OX-5 engine. The flight was very exhilarating; I felt quite at home in the open cockpit. The stick and rudder pedals worked just as I had expected they would. The only thing I didn't like was the roughness of the wheat field when we landed.

For the next several days I was able to keep my excursions under cover and I got in more lessons. But then my euphoric expression gave me away and I had to confess this new adventure to my parents. Their reprimand was not too harsh; in fact I got permission to continue my flying lessons, with the provision that I find a reputable school with modern equipment.

I did some investigating and found a bona fide flying school, the Naval Air Station at Glenview. The school was an adjunct of the Air Station and used Navy pilots and Navy training planes for instruction. My instructor had been a member of the Navy Stunt Team and after I soloed, I was given a chance to learn all the acrobatics that the Curtiss Fledgling was capable of. I now had to wait until my sixteenth birthday before I could get my pilot's license.

What did you like best about flying?

The acrobatics were exciting, but the flying I loved best was done in a tiny plane, the Curtiss Junior. It was not much more than a power glider. It had a three-cylinder engine and the propeller mounted as a pusher in the rear of the single overhead wing. The open cockpit was in the very nose, ahead of everything else, with a 360-degree view. I would coax the little thing up as high as it would go, about eight thousand feet. I would throttle back the engine and glide among the clouds in almost complete silence, with a view of the world below, as though seen by an ancient flying god.

Did you continue flying?

No, there was no practical use for this skill at that time, and as it was too expensive to justify only for pleasure, I stopped flying as suddenly as I had started. However, the experience came in handy years later during World War II when I was designing automatic flight controls for the Navy's fighters and bombers.

So then did you get back to painting?

Yes, by this time I was seventeen and the urge to paint was reasserting itself. One day at the farm, when the blue sky over the pasture and creek was filled with beautiful clouds, I felt I had to capture that scene. I still had my paint box and colors but I had no canvas. So I "borrowed" (like Huck Finn and the watermelons) one of my grandmother's card tables. I took it to the pasture, opened two legs so it would sit at an angle, and painted "The Willows and Sky" directly on the cloth surface of the table.

I then made a copy of a Rembrandt at the Chicago Art Institute. Later I asked my father to let me paint his portrait. This was a major project, for it was the first portrait other than the Rembrandt copy that I had ever tried. Since the canvas was to be 56 inches high, I felt I needed an elaborate easel to hold it and spent more time building it than I did painting the portrait.

THE EVANSTON LIVING ROOM
THE PAINTING IS ALSON CLARK'S
"MALAGA HARBOR"

PHOTO AT CHRISTMAS 1923
Stokely (lower right), his two brothers and his father.
The large painting is by Lawton Parker, the small one is
Stokely's first painting, the facade of Notre Dame.

PORTRAIT OF HIS FATHER
BY STOKELY WEBSTER 1931

WHO WAS WHO IN AMERICA

WEBSTER, Henry Kitchell, author, Evanston Ill., Sept. 7 1975; s. Towner Keeney and Emma J. (Kitchell) W.; grad. Hamilton Coll. 1879, L.H.H., 1925; instructor rhetoric, Union Coll. 1897-98; m. Mary Ward Orth, Sept. 7, 1901; children —Henry Kitchell, Stokely, Roderick Sheldon. Author, The Short Line War (with Samuel Merwin), 1899; The Banker and the Bear; The story of a corner in land, 1900; Calumet 'K', 1901; Roger Drake, Captain of Industry, 1903, The Duke of Cameron Avenue, 1903; Trator and Loyalist, 1904; Con-rad John, 1907; The Whispering Man, 1908; A King in Khaki, 1909; The Sky Man, 1910; The Girl in the Other Seat, 1911; June Madness (play), prod. New York, Sept. 1912; The Ghost Girl, 1913; The Butterfly, 1914; The Real Adventure, 1916; The Painted Scene, 1916; The Thoroughbred, 1917; An American Family, 1918; Mary Wollaston, 1920; Real Life, 1921; Joseph Greer and His Daughter, 1922; The Innocents, 1924; The Corbin Necklace, 1926; Philopena, 1927; The Beginners, 1927;The Clock Strikes Two, 1928; The Quartz Eye, 1928; The Sealed Trunk, 1929; Who is the Next, 1931; Home Evanston, Ill. Died Dec. 8, 1932.

) K S

Literary Circle Mourns Webster

BY FANNY BUTCHER.

THE CHICAGO TRIBUNE
SATURDAY, DECEMBER 10, 1932
HENRY KITCHELL WEBSTER OBITUARY

Henry Kitchell Webster will be missed grievously by our little world of Chicago writers, of which he has for so long been a vital member. We will miss him for the genial, kindly, but trenchant eye with which he saw life and the foibles of mankind. We will miss him for the Olympian calm and amused detachment with which he watched our little local strifes. We will miss his sense of humor and the twinkle in his eye and in his voice as he would sing the incomparable absurdities of the Gilbert and Sullivan operas, when he was feeling especially at home. We will miss a poised, friendly human being, and there are so few in the world!

But the great world outside our small circle will miss one of the most interesting writers of the day. There has been, in his own home town, too facile a judgment of the skill of Henry Kitchell Webster. His vast popularity has overshadowed his rightful place as a literary artist.

A few years ago he was the most popular author of serials in America. He was largely instrumental in the great literary revolution of the generation, making best books "best sellers," and he has not had the credit due him for that missionary work.

For throughout his literary career he never compromised with popularity. He wrote the best book which it was in him to write, whether it was a light or serious novel, and popularity was a well-won laurel wreath, no thorny crown, to remind him of his literary transgressions.

As good pictures of contemporary life in the Middle West as have been done are to be found in Henry Kitchell Webster's books. "An American Family" was an epic of the region which produced him. The social scene, both in fact and in critical interpretation, lives in his novels.

He was twenty-four years old when he wrote his first novel, "Short Line War," with Samuel Merwin. Two years later they collaborated on another book, "Calumet K," which to this day is a classic of the grain business in Chicago. "Calumet K" was placed on the list of advisory reading by the Harvard Engineering School. Countless employers bought it to give to employees not so much because it was a true and faithful picture of an industry, but because there glowed through its pages the vivifying romance of business.

How many books he wrote during the fifty-seven years of his life I do not know, for he was a meticulous writer and I suspect that in the long months of despair over his work which every creative writer suffers, he must have destroyed great masses of his writing. But he had, during his lifetime, 29 books published and one play produced.

These books are in every mood, from serious social criticism to really charming and delightful mystery yarns. Most of them have the Middle West and especially Chicago for their background, but there is a Civil War novel, one about the West Indies, and his characters are by no means "stay at home"; they get about all over the face of the world.

The great public, outside of his friends, may find it interesting to know that he graduated from Hamilton College, NY, and taught school rhetoric for a year or so and that he has lived in Evanston all of his life except during those few years. But his friends will be too sad at his leaving them to care for anymore vital statistics than the one that his roots in our common soil bore the fruit of ideals, a strangely real honesty in his work and in his life, that he was a proud figure in Chicago's proud panorama.

Did you go to college after high school? Did you major in painting?

I went East to Yale in the fall of 1931. I was accepted into the School of Architecture. I had in no way forsaken painting as a career, but my father had, in a gentle way, tried to dissuade me from being a painter. He admired painters and two of his very good friends, Alson Clark and Lawton Parker, were successful painters. However, being a literary artist himself, he knew that any art can be a difficult way to earn a living. I studied architecture as a compromise. I guess my father wanted to be sure that I had the determination to paint and was not just romanticizing a lifestyle. He knew that if I really had the drive to paint, that no petty obstacles would stop me. Architecture was in the "arts" but probably a better way to make a living. I was in the same class as Eero Saarinen; we had almost adjacent drafting tables.

But you didn't stay at Yale to finish your degree?

No, in the summer of 1932 after an exploratory operation, it was discovered that my father had incurable cancer and had only a few months to live. This was the most traumatic shock I had ever received. I loved my father and found it hard to imagine the world without him. When it came time to go back to Yale, I decided to stay in Evanston and my father wanted me to stay. I enrolled at Northwestern University, allowing me to live at home. My father died in December of that year. Ten years before, when my grandfather had died, my father had written a small book as a "memoir" of his father's life. In it, speaking about himself and his father, he had written, "The three years between quitting teaching at Union College and my marriage in the fall of 1901 were the beginning of a real unsentimental friendship between us, which isn't, after all, the commonest thing in the world between father and son." I felt the same sort of relationship had developed with my father, but now it was tragically and prematurely ended.

Was it difficult to continue with your studies after your father died?

Oh, yes! I didn't want to continue at Northwestern, nor did I want to go back to Yale. I had never wanted to be an architect and in 1933, all except the most famous of them were starving—just as much as the painters! So why not starve for what I loved to do? My mother wanted me to finish college, so to please her, I enrolled at Chicago University as a philosophy major. I took a room at International House and came home to Evanston on weekends.

I made the trip back and forth to Evanston on the Illinois Central railroad. The tracks at that point are multi-rail, a main line, local lines, sidings and freight yards. It was possible to stand beside the motorman's booth and watch the tracks ahead. This was my habitual post on the train. The train went straight down the main track, at high speed, but sometimes it would, without slowing down, negotiate a series of switches to other lanes and back. It seemed to me that this was a model of real life. You could follow one lane or if you had cause, you could switch to another. As I stood behind my front window, watching the switch points rush past, I reached a decision. I was going to start my painting career at that moment, not several years from now! Philosophy was not going to be much help to my painting, and life was too short to waste any of it. The only problem I faced was how to tell my mother! I knew that she would be violently opposed to my dropping out of school, and at the same time, if I persisted, she would insist on helping me financially, which was just what I didn't want!

OLD CHICAGO WATERTOWER
1933

OGDON SLIP
1933

LAKE FRONT, RAILYARDS
1933

So what did you do?

I wanted to prove that I could support myself as a painter! I knew that my mother was not only talented, but also strong-willed and very persuasive. So I decided that the only way my plan would work was to make it a "fait accompli."

I hinted to my mother that something was about to happen, and then I just disappeared. I took my paint box, a couple of shirts and two weeks' allowance with me. I rented a hall bedroom, with kitchen privileges, on North Erie Street. I phoned my mother every week to let her know that I was all right, but I would not give her my address. And thus I started my career!

Each day, weather permitting, I painted a city scene on a ten-by-twelve canvas panel. I painted the freight yard on the waterfront, the Twelfth St. Station, the Chicago River, the Old Water-tower and many more. I cooked my breakfasts in the hall kitchenette next to my room and I discovered Mrs. Vogel's restaurant in the basement, under her store. She served meals for little or no money. I was able to swap many weeks of dinners for a screen I painted for her, to hide the entrance to the kitchen.

Despite the fact that this was the depths of the Great Depression, I was able to sell my little paintings at ten dollars each to the Art Department at Marshall Fields and Carson Pierie Scott department stores. After several months I had accumulated ten times the money I had started off with, so I felt that I could support myself as a painter. I returned to Evanston and my mother.

It was about this time, wasn't it, that you and Iva got married and moved to New York City?

Yes, it was! Iva had finished two seasons with the Chicago Opera Ballet Company. Mr. Oukrainsky, the director, had developed a great appreciation of her talent and advised her to start thinking about a concert career. We planned to go to New York, where I would become a painter and Iva a concert dancer. We were married in Hillsdale, Michigan, in August 1933 and arrived in New York a week later. We found a two-room apartment at 65 West 68th St. It was inexpensive, but still a lot more than my one room in Chicago.

As I had in Chicago, I painted on the street and in the parks, but I did not find the department store outlets I had in Chicago. I decided that I must get a job and I was lucky to find one at Schweitzer and Company, a Swiss firm that supplied designs to manufacturers of printed silk materials. Here I made watercolor designs, two or three a day, for silk prints for ladies' dresses. After a year of this, I discovered that my "best selling" designs were mostly of a type used for evening gowns. I also discovered that I could sell them "free-lance" directly to the silk printing houses. I left Schweitzer's and made my designs in the room of the apartment set aside as a studio. I now had time again in daylight hours to paint outdoors. Once a distinguished-looking gentleman dropped a quarter in my paint box, thinking me a "sidewalk painter." I also had time to sell the new paintings and was able to place a few with good Madison Avenue galleries. I received three or four hundred dollars each for them.

IVA WITH WINE GLASS

1 9 3 9

Photo by Peter Juley

How did Iva fare in pursuing her dance career?

Iva got a job doing her satire of an 1890s ballerina with a vaudeville show that toured New England for many weeks. This involved the pain of separation, but it could not be helped if we were going to pursue both our careers. When she was home in New York, Iva took daily ballet classes with Massine or Kobelloff or Madame Toscanini. She rented studios and engaged pianists to work on and enlarge her repertoire of dance satires.

You were also spending a lot of time in The Metropolitan Museum of Art.

Yes, I got a permit to copy paintings in the Museum, where I had a locker to keep my paintings and equipment. I spent many months there, teaching myself the techniques of "The Masters" by copying them.

In the spring of 1937 I saw a "How To" film in the Museum, which featured a painter named Wayman Adams, painting a portrait--from start to finish--in three and a half hours. I was sufficiently impressed to make inquiries. I discovered that Adams was a student of Robert Henri and that he taught a summer class in Elizabethtown, N.Y. I signed up and spent six weeks there that summer.

Adams' technique was a mixture of those of Henri and John Singer Sargent. Each Friday afternoon Adams painted a portrait in less than four hours while the class watched. The other days the pupils struggled to do the same thing, with little success. I felt, however, that I did profit from my work with Adams. I gained freedom of brushwork and I especially enjoyed watching his "fencer like" lunge while he was painting.

How did you come to return to Europe?

Iva kept enlarging her repertoire and finally tried it out before an audience in the small theater on the second floor of Carnegie Hall. It was very well received and the next day an agent, who had seen the show, called her to ask if she would like to be part of a show at The Scala in Berlin. The pay was good, but we were very hesitant. Hitler was in control in Germany and had imposed currency controls that allowed no money to leave the country except to buy munitions. Iva succeeded in negotiating with the German Impresario that her salary would be deposited in her New York bank, and that two round-trip tickets on the liners Europa and Bremen would be mailed to us. Iva agreed and signed the contract. Soon we were on the high seas!

New Year's Day in 1938 in Berlin was cold and gray. The military guards, stationed before all important buildings, were chilling when they barked, "Heil Hitler!" as you passed, and growled and hissed if you didn't return the statement with a stiff arm salute! The show at The Scala, however, was a huge success, with standing room only and thunderous applause. Crowds at the stage door and even in restaurants would seek Iva's autograph. I was backstage for many of the performances. One of the big events of the winter was the Press Ball. Iva was invited to do one of her numbers there, to entertain "the distinguished guests." She politely declined, because she knew that "the distinguished guests" were the Nazi bigwigs. The invitation was repeated the next day, delivered by a messenger carrying an automatic rifle. He made it quite clear that one did not refuse such an invitation! So of course she went! The affair was held in a circular room with the audience all around the edge and the performers doing their bits in the center. In the first row were seated most of the top Reich Ministers and Generals Goering, Goebbels and Himmler, to name a few. Hitler was supposed to be there, but had a last-minute change of plans. Iva liked to muse afterward about how she might have changed history if she could have smuggled a machine gun in under her ballet skirt and let it run while she executed a dozen pirouettes.

I still have a copy of a letter that I wrote at the time to my brother Kitchell and his wife Madeline.

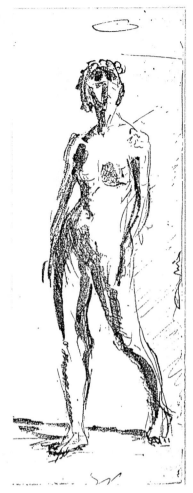

Berlin, January 30, 1938

Hello Kitch, Hello Madie:

Iva had to leave at this point to go on for the finale. I have just come in from seeing a most remarkable sight! Will tell you about it. Today is the 30th of January and the fifth anniversary of the present regime. We couldn't have failed to know that something was going on, for there are red swastika flags flying on every roof and from every window, and even on the trolley poles of the streetcars. The main streets are decorated, at the public expense, with enormous flags that .. *reach from the third floor of the buildings almost to the street, all the most brilliant red that cloth can be dyed.*

We didn't know though (not being able to make much of the papers) what a celebration they were planning. I went downtown about 8 o'clock, thinking to go to the opera, and found the streets crowded, like Broadway on New Year's Eve. The opera and apparently everything else was "*Ausverkauft.*"

Then, walking down a long, dark street, I saw torches (a steady stream of them) going across the "T" head at the end of it. I worked my way through the crowd till I was near the end. About 15 minutes had elapsed, and still the steady stream of torches was passing, and I could hear the regular thud of marching troops.

There was no such thing as getting nearer in that street, but knowing something of the geography of this part of the city, I figured out where the parade was heading and went there by a different route. A great square in front of the Government buildings was also hung on all four sides with these long red flags, and the flags spotlighted with powerful army searchlights, so that the square glowed with a red light! And over the heads of the crowd, on the far side of the square—again the stream of torches and drums beating time for the march--and above on a balcony, were Hitler and his generals.

I climbed part way up a statue to see better. I don't know how long the procession had been passing the reviewing stand before I came, or how long it lasted after I left, but the part that I did watch pass must have been nearly a mile long and the column was about 25 men wide, and every man carried a torch and marched the goose-step. In short it was "formidable"! Iva is ready to go now . . . *so I will stop.*

Goodbye, Love

Stokely

PARIS, 1938

WERE YOU ABLE TO PAINT WHILE YOU WERE IN GERMANY?

Yes, when I wasn't at the theater, I rented a studio and painted some portraits, one of them the American singer Janet Fairbank. I also studied drawing in a life class in Berlin.

In February The Scala Show moved to the Deutches Theater in Munich. In early March the weather turned beautiful and on days when there was no matinee we would bicycle out into the countryside. We had the joy of a trip to Oberammergau and Garmisch, in the lovely Bavarian Alps.

OTHER THAN IVA'S COMMAND PERFORMANCE, DID YOU HAVE A DIRECT SENSE OF WHAT WAS GOING ON IN GERMANY AT THAT TIME?

Oh, there was trouble in the air everywhere. You could sense it in the tenseness of the troops. We were forewarned by our friend Sigrid Schultz, the German correspondent of the Chicago Daily News, that war was imminent, and that we should leave if we could. Iva's contracted engagement had run out; she was only staying on because the show kept running to good houses. We decided to leave, but there was a problem. The police had Iva's passport and were not inclined to give it up. We spent hours waiting in the police headquarters while she was told over and over (just like the scene in Menotti's The Consul) "just one more signature required."

SO WHAT DID YOU DO?

We finally thought of a solution. We went to the American Consul and got Iva included on my passport. We packed what we had at the theater and the "pension" and tried to get a taxi to take us to the station. No luck! We had been so busy packing that we had missed the clamor on the radio and loudspeakers. The "Anschluss," the takeover of Austria, had started! All cabs had been requisitioned to carry troops to the front! Then the drone of planes overhead started and kept up for what seemed hours. We were completely astonished! I could not believe that there were that many airplanes in the whole world. Having been a pilot, I had a better idea about war planes than most Americans had.

I knew at that moment that there would be a war and that America would have to be in it. We had better not waste any time getting an air force that could cope with what I was looking at! We did get our baggage to the station in a cart, pulled by a man. We were able to buy tickets to Italy and got on the train. It progressed safely as far as Innsbruck. There, it was stopped by German troops who had arrived hours before. After a three-hour delay, with many passengers on the train being questioned and removed, the train was allowed to proceed. Within a few hours it passed through the Brenner Gorge and into Italy. We breathed a great sigh of relief! We felt a sense of freedom from tension that had been building up! The next day it became apparent that no country was prepared to fight over the loss of Austria, and the world got another temporary reprieve from the looming war.

DID YOU RETURN HOME TO THE UNITED STATES RIGHT AWAY?

No, I had promised to show Iva the wonderful places in Europe that had so captivated me fifteen years before. First on the list was Venice. We saw all the same cities and natural wonders that I had seen as a child of ten. When we got to Paris, I bought a new paint box and started to paint. I did a painting of the Champs Élysées (which is now in the collection of the Smithsonian National Museum of American Art) and the Terrace at St. Germain-En-Laye, now at the Phillips Collection, also in Washington, DC.

WERE YOU AWARE OF MODERNIST ART IN EUROPE AND THE WORK OF PICASSO AND BRAQUE?

Yes, they were center stage in Paris, even when I was there as a young boy. But I was not too intrigued.

WHY NOT? WHAT DID INTEREST YOU?

Actually I found Picasso "formidable," in fact thrilling, but I didn't see how his personal approach was going to help me any in capturing the subtle beauty in nature that intrigued me. I had found a way to paint, related to Impressionism, that allowed me to capture my own vision of the world and I didn't want to be distracted.

AS YOU WERE AWARE OF THE IMMINENCE OF WAR, WHAT DID YOU DO?

I was so concerned with getting the warning back to America about preparing for a certain conflict with the German Airforce, that we cut our travels short and sailed home to New York. We found, however, that our warnings were not welcomed. They fell on either deaf or hostile ears. Most Americans at that time were more concerned with staying out of involvement in Europe than they were about the threatening reality of the situation!

WAS IT DIFFICULT TO RETURN TO NEW YORK AND RESUME YOUR CAREER?

No! I was lucky. I started showing my paintings to galleries and was pleased to find that I was warmly received at the O'Toole Gallery in Manhattan. James St. Lawrence O'Toole had worked for years as a representative of Duveen Brothers in London and New York. At that moment of time he was opening his own gallery on East 51st Street. He gave me his biggest room for the opening exhibition of the new gallery! Most of the other rooms contained "Old Masters" on consignment, or collected over the years by O'Toole. My exhibition attracted praise from the critics of the three major New York newspapers. One of them commented that "he should be a sure success where taste calls for something elegant."

I was now selling paintings and Iva and I had a studio with a skylight on East 37th Street. Everything was going well, but I couldn't get that sight of a sky full of German fighters and bombers out of my mind. I decided that I could paint on weekends and that I would try to achieve something personally about our war plane production.

I got a shop job at the Grumman Aircraft Engineering Co. at Bethpage, Long Island. We gave up the studio and found an apartment near the plant. At Grumman there *was* an appreciation of the urgency for greater production. They were suppliers to the U.S. Navy and the Navy was aware of our deficiency, compared with Nazi Germany. Columbia University had set up an outpost program, in the plant, to upgrade engineers in airplane design. I was able to take advantage of these night courses, while I was working in the shop, and soon I was transferred to the engineering department.

Before the bombing of Pearl Harbor, in 1941, I was designing control and automatic systems for the new Grumman fighter, the F6F. After Pearl Harbor, almost unlimited funds were available to speed design and production of these planes. Our workload increased to twelve and sixteen hours a day, seven days a week. Something else happened, that was unforgettable, suddenly America was united and determined. There was an urgency in the air. Our on-time delivery of carrier airplanes to the Pacific Fleet was an important element that made it possible for Admiral Nimitz to launch his bold surprise attack on the Japanese at Midway. The enemy fleet out-numbered ours by more than two to one, but the element of surprise and the skill of our pilots enabled us to sink four of their large carriers, to the loss of one of ours. From that point it was nothing but downhill for the Japanese.

TELL US MORE ABOUT YOUR LIFE DURING THOSE GRUMMAN YEARS.

It was through Grumman that Iva and I met Norman and Audrey Coutant. Norman was of Scotch-Irish and Huguenot descent. His family had roots in Normandy and La Rochelle in France and had land grants in New Rochelle, NY. Audrey was a great, great granddaughter of Heinrich Lenz, the author of "Lenz's Law" that defined the operation of electrical generators. Norman was one of the top test pilots for Grumman. Since I had designed much of the auto-pilot equipment for the TBF, I had had frequent occasion to ride along on his test flights of this equipment. Norman and I developed an appreciation of each other's abilities, which turned into a lasting friendship. Iva and Audrey soon became best friends and Iva and I became godparents to the Coutant children.

WERE YOU ABLE TO RESUME YOUR PAINTING AFTER THE WAR?

THE GARGOYLES, NORTH TOWER, NOTRE DAME de PARIS, 1938

Yes, I left Grumman and was able to sub-lease George Luks' old studio on East 22nd St. in Manhattan. The studio was the entire top floor. It was eighty feet long by twenty-five feet wide and twenty feet high, with three skylights. It adjoined another studio building on 23rd Street, connected to it by a little roof garden. One day it became apparent that the tenants in the other building were moving out. I was able to rent it before it went on the market. This was advantageous, for there was an elevator, which was something lacking in the first studio. It had a magnificent skylight, looking out over Madison Square.

I was doing portraits and preparing paintings for another New York exhibition. The problem was that during the war, James O'Toole had closed his establishment and accepted a commission in the Navy. Now that he was out of the service, he was selling his "Old Masters" by appointment from his townhouse, but he did not reopen the gallery. Also, the group of art critics who had found my work so interesting had been replaced by a new group, who seemed to feel that painting, to be praiseworthy, had to be "different" with no tie to tradition. As I mentioned earlier, I felt no desire to change my way of painting! It expressed what I wanted it to and I thought that to make a painting different, just to be different, was dishonest.

SO WHAT DID YOU DO THEN?

The inventor Theodore Kenyon, with whom I had worked closely at Grumman, had received financial backing from a Boston entrepreneur to start a company for building gyroscopic guidance equipment for missiles. He asked me to join him in the venture as chief designer. I reluctantly agreed to give Kenyon three days a week at his company in Huntington, L.I. Iva and I bought a house in Huntington and lived there part time, spending our weekends in the New York studio.

THEN YOU HAD A GREAT CATASTROPHE?

THE NEW YORK STUDIO

I sure did! On January 5, 1952, the New York studio building burned to the ground! More than sixty of the latest of my paintings were destroyed! Jacques Lipschitz, who had the studio above mine, lost many works in Pleistocene, and his bronzes were subsequently found in the basement!

THIS MUST HAVE BEEN EXTREMELY TRAUMATIC FOR YOU.

I abandoned any thought of another exhibition. Iva and I moved to Huntington full time and I agreed to devote more time to the Gyroscope Company. I continued to paint in the Huntington studio, but for the next five years considerable effort had to be devoted to "Gyro-mechanisms." After four years I was elected president of the company. A year later, I felt I could recommend that the Boston owners accept a generous offer from the Norden Company to purchase the operation. The owners recouped their investment many times over. I was tired of the responsibility of meeting weekly payrolls and was delighted to get back to painting full time.

WERE YOU ABLE, IN FACT, TO PAINT FULL TIME?

Eventually, but first I returned for a few years to the Grumman Corporation, where I worked as an "Assistant to the President." It was only a staff job, but one that offered very interesting insight into the operation of a huge industry.

Our house in Huntington had been a large barn on the Jay Gould estate. I bought it on ten acres of woodland in 1950, and converted it into a residence and a studio. The studio had one 30-foot wall, all mirrored, and a 16-foot-high north window, so it made an excellent dance studio as well as one for painting. Iva and I worked here for thirty years.

After Iva retired from the stage, she taught ballet, for she loved activity and she loved children. Iva and I adopted one of her most talented students, Stephanie Turner. We gave many parties for New Year's Eve and birthdays and square dances which were held in the studio, with the Coutants and dozens of friends from Grumman.

HOW DID YOU AND AUDREY COME TO MARRY?

THE TERRACE   THE STUDIO

Her husband, Norman Coutant, died of a heart attack in 1972. In 1980 Iva and I moved to Boca Raton, Florida, in the hope that the change would alleviate severe allergies that Iva had developed. The change did not help her and neither did a subsequent move to an oceanside house, north of Daytona. In November 1983, soon after we had celebrated our 50th wedding anniversary, Iva suffered a massive stroke and died.

I found myself alone, after many happy years of marriage. It seemed most natural to ask Audrey to marry me since she too was alone. She accepted and we were married in May 1984.

Audrey had always been a passionate believer in my paintings and we now worked together, organizing exhibitions and catalogues. We also decided to move back to New England. We found another barn that we could convert into a studio home on the Connecticut shore. For the last fourteen years we've spent winters there and summers traveling on painting trips all over Europe.

How would you describe your working together with Audrey?

For several years, I watched in awe as Audrey demonstrated time and time again that she understood instinctively what was good and not good about my paintings. One day, I said to her, "You should paint too." In my opinion, the only difficult part of being a painter, is in being able to see the paintable. The technique is the easy part. I bought her a French easel paint box like mine and gave her a few hints about technique. Now we go painting together, whether it be in Connecticut or France, and usually paint the same motif.

Can you tell me anything about your technique?

I expected that you were going to ask me that. I have jotted down a few notes that you might want to include in this record. They are a very abbreviated account of one of my working methods. But first let me mention my thoughts about technique, as it applies to painting. It is of course an important element in making a good painting but it is not, in my opinion, the most important. The most important ingredient, I think, is the ability to see the picture, to recognize what will make a good painting.

I think that with that we had better call it a day!

Lowery, I am really glad that you have questioned me and that your questions and the search for the old photographs have stirred my memory of times so long ago. They were happy times and it is fun to bring them back to mind and conjure up many more visions than we were able to discuss. Perhaps another time?

Editor's note: Webster's comments on technique appear on page 364.

VENICE 1938

PREPARATION AND STUDIES

by

HAROLD C. SCHONBERG

American Critic, Former Student of Kuniyoshi,
Cultural Correspondent of the New York Times

In 1784 Mozart became friendly with a pianist named Georg Fredrich Richter.   Richter watched Mozart play and kept on saying, "Great God! How hard I work and sweat, and yet win no applause, and to you, my friend, it is all child's play."

Mozart had the perfect answer. "Yes," he said, "I too had to work hard, so as not to have to work hard any longer."

For Mozart, perhaps the most gifted musician who ever lived, realized that talent and not even genius are enough. Talent has to be honed from the beginning. That means work, total dedication, complete immersion in the art from childhood on.

So it has been with Stokely Webster. He paints fluently and easily, with a formidable technique and style that make painting seem like child's play. But he too had to work hard so as not to have to work hard any longer. He started as a nine-year-old in Paris, drawing and painting his impressions. As a student (though he largely has been self-taught) he spent hours upon hours in museums all over the world, copying Old Masters—the equivalent of finger exercises for an instrumentalist.

That work gave him a technique in which messages from the eye immediately translated into orders to hand and brush and those orders are instantly obeyed. Stokely Webster is a fast painter. He is also a lyric painter. The essence of lyricism is to catch an emotion on the wing, fixing it for all eternity. Lyricism does not necessarily involve the Big Statement (though in some cases it can). Rather it aims at a highly personal statement, expressed intimately, rapidly, accurately, poetically—A Chopin étude, as opposed to a symphony, an improvisation as opposed to a treatise.

Thus he has to paint fast. By itself, to paint fast means nothing. But to paint fast with absolute security, with style and personality, is an ability reserved only for superb technicians. Webster was once asked, in a radio interview, about his speed. "What is the quickest and best way to get the effects that I want to get? Quickness is important because when you paint outdoors the way I do, the sun changes, shadows change and unless you can get it down fairly quickly, you get a mishmash of different lighting effects instead of the one you really liked." His work illustrates Occam's law: simplicity is best. One thing can be said about any Webster painting—it is never overworked, never fussy.

SIR PERCIVAL VIVIAN, 1937

Stokely Webster as a child developed an admiration and love for the Impressionists. Monet is the name that most frequently springs to his lips. Never has he wavered from that first great overwhelming influence. In the great days of Abstract Expressionism and the succeeding post war styles that became so immensely popular (and are now period curiosities) he remained an Impressionist—a realist, if you will. His painting continued to be rooted in the figure, in nature, in what he sees. Definitely he was old-fashioned, with such old-fashioned notions as the conviction that an artist has to know how to draw, or that an artist has to convey emotion in his paintings. "It seems to me," he once said of Abstract Expressionism, "that it is too limited to be real art." Today he is not so old-fashioned. Realism has returned. Everywhere realism has returned. Once again artists in all fields—even avant-garde artists—-look to the past, no longer scorning the realism that was anathema only a short time ago.

But if Webster is an Impressionist, he has filtered Impressionism through his experience and developed a highly individual style. His fast moving brush eliminates all unessentials. Everything is pared down almost to an Idea in the Platonic sense. Nor has he ever been a flamboyant colorist. Yet light is an animating factor of his work, and in his paintings light always leaps from the canvas.

He is a realist who never tells a story in his paintings. He never preaches, he is not a social commentator, he has no particular theories about painting aside from a conviction that a picture should have life and poetry. He just paints! He uses colors and forms to express things as they are; and since he is an imaginative painter as well as a technician, he has a lyric vision that also expresses himself as well as what he sees.

THE
PLATES

PARIS

SAINT GERMAIN-EN-LAYE

1923

Painted when the artist was ten years old

PLATE I   57

CHATEAU OF FRANCIS THE FIRST

1923

Conté drawing on back of Plate 1, Age ten

PLATE 2

CHAMPS ÉLYSÉES

1938

National Museum of American Art, Smithsonian Institution

PLATE 3

PONT NEUF

1969

PLATE 4

QUAI DU LOUVRE

1985

PLATE 5

UNDER THE EIFFEL TOWER

1953

PLATE 6

PLACE FURSTENBERG

1990

PLATE 7

METRO LATOUR-MAUBOURG

1970

Museum of Fine Arts, St. Petersburg, Florida

PLATE 8

SQUARE HENRI GALLI

1971

PLATE 9

65

LUXEMBOURG GARDENS
1960

PLATE 10

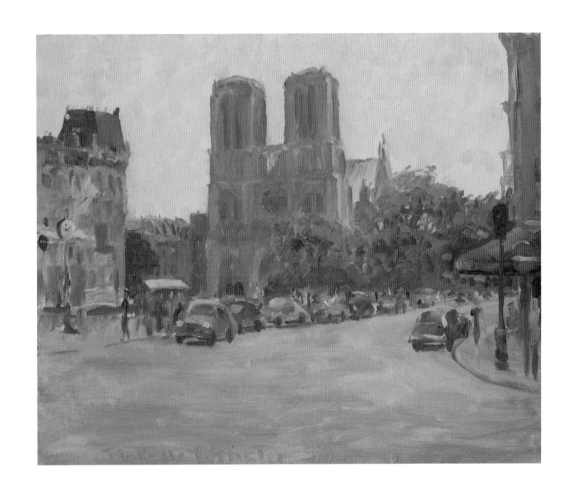

NOTRE DAME
1977

PLATE II   67

FACADE, NOTRE DAME

1994

PLATE 12

NOTRE DAME

1993

PLATE 13

69

TUILLERIES POND
1979

PLATE 14

RAINY DAY IN PARIS

1984

PLATE 15   71

NOTRE DAME DE PARIS

1996

PLATE 16

PONT NEUF
1988

PLATE 17

CHAMPS ÉLYSÉES
1995

PLATE 18

PARK IN PARIS

1994

PLATE 19

QUAI DE MONTEBELLO
1989

PLATE 20

ALLÉE THOMY THIERRY
1995

PLATE 21

PONT D'IÉNA
1995

PLATE 22

SACRÉ COEUR

1989

PLATE 23

MEDICI FOUNTAIN, LUXEMBOURG GARDENS
1992

PLATE 24

MEDICI FOUNTAIN, LUXEMBOURG GARDENS
1990

PLATE 25

NOTRE DAME IN STORM
1988

PLATE 26

THE SEINE, INSTITUT DES ARTS
1990

PLATE 27

RUE ST. LAZARE

1988

PLATE 28

PANTHÉON FROM ILE ST. LOUIS
1988

PLATE 29   85

LUXEMBOURG GARDENS AND THE PANTHÉON
1987

PLATE 30

ALLÉE IN THE LUXEMBOURG GARDENS
1985

PLATE 31

LUXEMBOURG GARDENS AND POND
1984

PLATE 32

LUXEMBOURG POND AND FOUNTAIN
1988

PLATE 33

89

PONT ROYAL AND THE LOUVRE
1989

PLATE 34

THE LOUVRE
1988

PLATE 35

AVENUE DES INVALIDES

1979

PLATE 36

BOULEVARD DE GRENELLE
1959

PLATE 37

QUAI DE LA CONFÉRENCE

1979

PLATE 38

TUILLERIES POND
1979

PLATE 39

VERSAILLES
1988

PLATE 40

PARC ST. CLOUD
1995

PLATE 41

FOUNTAIN IN GRASSE

1990

The Collection of President and Mrs. Ronald Reagan

98

PLATE 42

PARC MONCEAU
1994

PLATE 43
99

AVENUE DE BRETEUIL

1998

PLATE 44

PLACE DUPLEIX

1979

PLATE 45

PARK IN POISSY

1994

PLATE 46

FRENCH COUNTRYSIDE

THE SEINE NEAR GIVERNY

1994

PLATE 47

CASSIS

1953

PLATE 48

ÉTRETAT

1992

PLATE 49

STORM AT ÉTRETAT

1992

PLATE 50

SAINT YON

1992

PLATE 51

MORET

1992

PLATE 52

AVIGNON

1994

PLATE 53

VINEYARD OVER CASSIS
1987

PLATE 54

MORET SUR LOING

1995

PLATE 55

POPLARS ON THE ÉSSONE
1994

PLATE 56

ORANGERIE, STRASBOURG

1993

PLATE 57

COURS MIRABEAU, AIX-EN-PROVENCE
1990

PLATE 58   115

ST. PIERRE, MONTFORD L'AMAURY

1991

PLATE 59

PONT DU LOUP

1991

PLATE 60

FARM IN THE ILE DE FRANCE

1994

PLATE 61

ROAD IN THE ILE DE FRANCE
1994

PLATE 62

CASTLE IN MANDELIEU

1992

PLATE 63

PLACE DU FORUM, ARLES

1992

PLATE 64

SOISSY SUR ÉCOLE
1992

PLATE 65

ALPHONSE DAUDET STATUE
1990

PLATE 66

123

THE SEINE AT HONFLEUR

1985

PLATE 67

QUAI AT LA CIOTAT

1 9 8 5

PLATE 68

LA CIOTAT

1996

PLATE 69

CAFÉ DES ARTS, ST. TROPEZ
1991

PLATE 70

CHATEAU FONTCREUSE
1991

PLATE 71

BESANCON
1994

PLATE 72

FORUM IN ARLES

1991

PLATE 73

LILLA CABOT PERRY STUDIO

1992

PLATE 74

PROMENADE AT GRASSE
1990

PLATE 75

PARK IN MENTON
1990

PLATE 76

CAFÉ TERMINUS

1992

PLATE 77

STREET IN NIMES

1996

PLATE 78

RAIN IN THE AUVERGNE

1979

136   PLATE 79

STUDIO IN GOURDON

1992

The Collection of General and Mrs. William Odom

PLATE 80

137

CANAL IN STRASBOURG

1993

PLATE 81

RIVER IN ANNECY

1992

PLATE 82

MOULIN DE LA PLANCHE

1984

PLATE 83

FOUNTAIN IN CASSIS
1969

PLATE 84

ORÁNGERIE, STRASBOURG

1996

PLATE 85

JET D'EAU, ORANGERIE

1996

PLATE 86

CARROUSEL IN NÎMES

1991

PLATE 87

THE SEINE AND PONT ALEXANDRE TROIS
1996

PLATE 88

PONT ST. MICHEL

1974

PLATE 89

ÉGLISE, FONTENAY MAUVOISIN

1992

PLATE 90

COGNES SUR LOIRE

1971

PLATE 91

RAINBOW PASS NORTH OF PAMPLONA

1970

PLATE 92

RED BARNS NEAR ÉPINAL

1971

PLATE 93

A ROAD IN FRANCE

1960

PLATE 94   151

SAINT ELIZABETH BRIDGE, BRUGGES
1989

PLATE 95

PARK IN BRUGGES

1989

PLATE 96

DOCK AT CHERBOURG
1971

PLATE 97

EARLY PAINTINGS

WILLOWS AND SKY

1929

PLATE 98

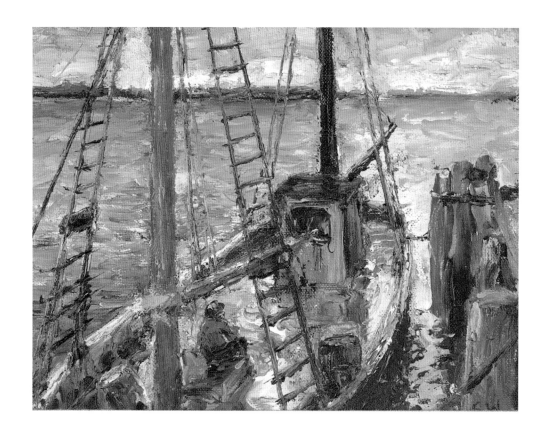

PROVINCETOWN BOAT

1930

PLATE 99

PROVINCETOWN TREE

1930

PLATE 100

159

CHICAGO WATERTOWER

1933

PLATE 101

COLUMBUS CIRCLE

1935

PLATE 102

161

CHICAGO RAILYARD

1933

The Illinois State Museum, Springfield, Illinois

PLATE 103

BROOKLYN BRIDGE

1936

PLATE 104

MADISON SQUARE
1950

PLATE 105

HOUSE AT OREGON, ILLINOIS
1933

PLATE 106

SELF PORTRAIT IN CAPE

1934

PLATE 107

IVA WITH CAMEO

1937

PLATE 108

IVA

1934

PLATE 109

SELF PORTRAIT
1934

PLATE 110

IVA LOOKING OVER SHOULDER
1951

PLATE III

IVA IN WHITE FRILL BLOUSE
1937

PLATE 112

CENTRAL PARK AT SEVENTH AVENUE
1939

PLATE 113

CENTRAL PARK, WEST DRIVE

1937

The Collection of Ronald Pisano

PLATE 114

IVA WITH WINE GLASS
1938

PLATE 115

MARIA THERESA ACUNA
1950

PLATE 116   175

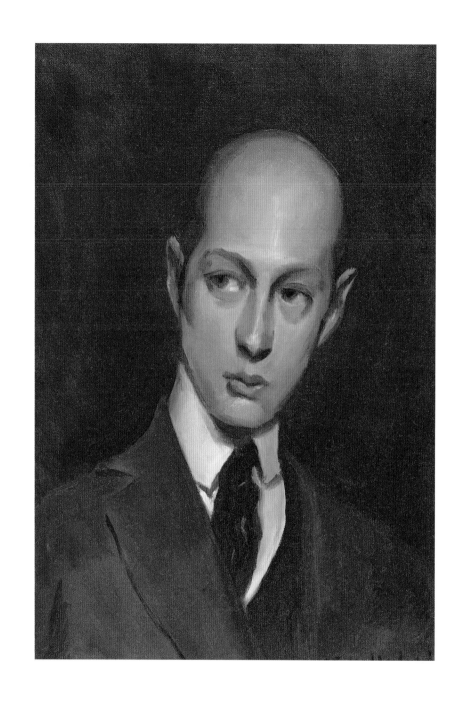

HUGH NORTON

1938

PLATE 117

HELEN DERMOLINSKA

1950

PLATE 118

LITTLE NECK BAY

1945

PLATE 119

FRUIT BOWL

1949

PLATE 120

UNIVERSITY CLUB

1940

The Daytona Museum of Arts, Florida

PLATE 121

TIMES SQUARE, SUNDAY MORNING
1940

The Museum of the City of New York

PLATE 122

SELF PORTRAIT WITH PIPE

1937

The Denver Museum of Art

PLATE 123

JOSSEY WITH GLASS
1937

PLATE 124

BETS ON BEACH
1945

PLATE 125

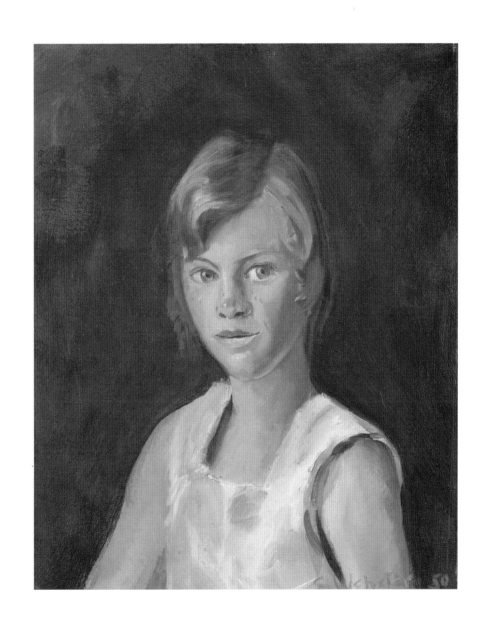

BETS

1950

PLATE 126

185

IVA, IN "BEFORE THE BALL"

1949

PLATE 127

MODEL RESTING

1949

The Phillips Collection, Washington, DC

PLATE 128

STORM ON SOUTH SHORE
1944

CENTRAL PARK SOUTH

1943

Cornell Art Center, Winter Park, Florida

PLATE 130

PEGGY KORN

1950

The Collection of Peggy Harriman Korn

PLATE 131

IVA IN BLACK VELVET DRESS

1938

The High Museum of Art, Atlanta, Georgia

PLATE 132

KEY WEST STREET
1949

PLATE 133

HAVANA HARBOR

1949

The Daytona Museum of Art, Florida

PLATE 134

IVA IN STRAW HAT
1950

PLATE 135

IVA
1945

PLATE 136

JONES BEACH
1948

PLATE 137

THE BEACH

1945

The Indianapolis Museum of Art, Indiana

PLATE 138

IVA ·AND HARVEY, 23RD STREET STUDIO
1951

PLATE 139

MADISON SQUARE PARK

1949

The Frye Museum, Seattle, Washington

PLATE 140   199

CUT GLASS
1949

PLATE 141

IVA IN FLOWER HAT

1945

Indianapolis Museum of Art, Indiana

PLATE 142

IVA AS A CHORUS GIRL

1945

The Parrish Museum, Southampton, New York

PLATE 143

THE SEA CAPTAIN
1950

PLATE 144   203

MARY HUTCHINSON
1936

PLATE 145

KIRSTEN OLSEN
1950

PLATE 146

FIFTH AVENUE AT CENTRAL PARK
1936

PLATE 147

THREE LIMP ROSES

1967

PLATE 148

AFRICAN VIOLETS

1968

PLATE 149

PORT WASHINGTON

1941

PLATE 150

CARROUSEL
1940

PLATE 151

CARRIAGE IN THE PARK
1938

PLATE 152

211

IVA ON BALCONY

1953

PLATE 153

IVA IN WHITE LEOTARD

1959

PLATE 154

STEPHIE

1953

PLATE 155

THE BLUE TIGHTS
1961

PLATE 156

COMPOTE WITH FRUIT

1966

The Collection of Ron Pisano

216   PLATE 157

STILL LIFE WITH DECORATED VASE
1971

PLATE 158

FRENCH BREAD AND BOTTLE

1965

PLATE 159

CARAFE ON TRAY

1967

PLATE 160

219

NEW YORK

NIAGARA FALLS

1992

Albright-Knox Art Gallery, Buffalo, New York

PLATE 161

FIFTH AVENUE SOUTH FROM THE METROPOLITAN
1987

PLATE 162

FIFTH AVENUE AT THE METROPOLITAN
1987

PLATE 163

THE POND AT CENTRAL PARK
1985

PLATE 164

THE PLAZA FOUNTAIN
1985

PLATE 165

225

FIFTH AVENUE AT 60TH STREET

1972

PLATE 166

THE SAILBOAT POND
1983

PLATE 167   227

FIFTH AVENUE BY THE PARK
1983

PLATE 168

THE GUGGENHEIM MUSEUM
1987

PLATE 169

CENTRAL PARK AT SEVENTH AVENUE
1985

PLATE 170

THE POND, CENTRAL PARK

1988

PLATE 171

THE PLAZA FROM 61ST STREET
1987

PLATE 172

THE PLAZA FROM 60TH STREET
1987

PLATE 173

FIFTH AVENUE, LOOKING NORTH
1985

PLATE 174

ENTRANCE TO THE PARK
1985

PLATE 175

BROADWAY AT COLUMBUS AVENUE

1983

Collection of Harold C. Schonberg

236   PLATE 176

THE POND, LOOKING EAST
1987

PLATE 177

BROOKLYN BRIDGE

1 9 8 3

The Collection of Austin Kiplinger

PLATE 178

FIFTH AVENUE, THE GUGGENHEIM
1987

PLATE 179

WILSON HARBOR
1986

240 PLATE 180

SANDY HARBOR
1987

PLATE 181

FIFTH AVENUE WITH CARRIAGE
1987

PLATE 182

LONDON

HOUSES OF PARLIAMENT

1996

PLATE 183

WESTMINSTER BRIDGE

1992

The Collection of Mr. and Mrs. Richard Kelly

PLATE 184

HOUSES OF PARLIAMENT
1992

PLATE 185

WESTMINSTER BRIDGE

1989

PLATE 186

TOWER BRIDGE

1996

PLATE 187

FARM IN BEDFORDSHIRE

1989

PLATE 188

RIVER AT CAMBRIDGE
1989

PLATE 189

251

BATH ON AVON

1989

PLATE 190

BRIDGES ON THE CAM RIVER

1989

PLATE 191

BRIDGE IN CAMBRIDGE

1984

PLATE 192

BRIDGE OF SIGHS
1989

PLATE 193

PUNTS ON THE CAM RIVER
1989

PLATE 194

BRIDGE ON THE CAM RIVER
1989

PLATE 195

WATERMILL IN WALES

1989

PLATE 196

SERPENTINE AT HYDE PARK

1989

PLATE 197

259

BRIDGE AT TOTNES

1995

PLATE 198

VENICE

PIAZZA S. MARCO
1993

PLATE 199   263

THREE PALACES ON THE GRAND CANAL
1990

PLATE 200

SANTA MARIA DELLA SALUTE
1992

PLATE 201

PUNTA DELLA DOGANA

1992

PLATE 202

DOGES PALACE

1996

PLATE 203

PALACES ON THE GRAND CANAL
1990

PLATE 204

PIAZETTA S. MARCO
1992

PLATE 205   269

GONDOLA ON A SIDE CANAL

1991

PLATE 206

LOGGIA IN VENICE
1991

PLATE 207

GRAND CANAL. VENICE

1990

PLATE 208

CHIESA DELLA SALUTE
1990

PLATE 209

273

LA SALUTE

1994

PLATE 210

VENICE, BRIDGE OF SIGHS
1994

PLATE 211

C'A DA MOSTA

1991

PLATE 212

PALACE IN VENICE
1990

PLATE 213

THE RIALTO BRIDGE
1992

PLATE 214

THE RIALTO BRIDGE, VENICE
1990

PLATE 215

S. GIORGIO MAGGIORE
1990

PLATE 216

CAMPANILE AND DOGES PALACE
1990

PLATE 217

S. GIORGIO MAGGIORE AT DUSK
1996

PLATE 218

ENTRANCE TO THE GRAND CANAL

1996

PLATE 219

BACINO S. MARCO

1996

　　　　　PLATE 220

STORM IN VENICE

1992

PLATE 221

THE SEA

THE BEACH AT DEAUVILLE

1975

PLATE 222

FIRE ISLAND BEACH

1980

PLATE 223

THE FIRE ISLAND BEACH

1994

PLATE 224

THE BEACH AT ORMOND

1984

PLATE 225

HALIFAX RIVER, SEA BREEZE PARK

1984

PLATE 226

THE BEACH AT ORMOND BY THE SEA
1985

PLATE 227

SAILBOATS ON BEACH IN FOG
1978

PLATE 228

BEACH AT SUNSET

1976

PLATE 229

SASCO BEACH
1985

PLATE 230

ROCKS AT WASHINGTON OAKS
1983

PLATE 231

THE GULFSTREAM AT WASHINGTON OAKS
1995

PLATE 231

SPANISH BEACH

1988

The Collection of Jon Monson

PLATE 233

BOATS AT NOANK

1998

PLATE 234

SAUGATUCK SHORES

1995

PLATE 235

WEST CHOP, MARTHA'S VINEYARD
1989

PLATE 236

RIVERSIDE AT NOANK

1986

PLATE 237

STRATFORD BRIDGE

1987

PLATE 238

BEACH AT MADISON

1987

PLATE 239

SHINNECOCK INLET

1976

PLATE 240

THE WAVE
1984

PLATE 241

ROUGH SEA

1988

PLATE 242

THE ROAD AT DUSK

1 9 8 4

PLATE 243

PORTRAITS
AND
STILL-LIFES

YELLOW MUMS

1992

PLATE 244

MUGUET ET RHODODENDRON

1991

PLATE 245

PINK ROSES

1992

PLATE 246

SANDRA

1974

PLATE 247

AUDREY

1986

PLATE 248

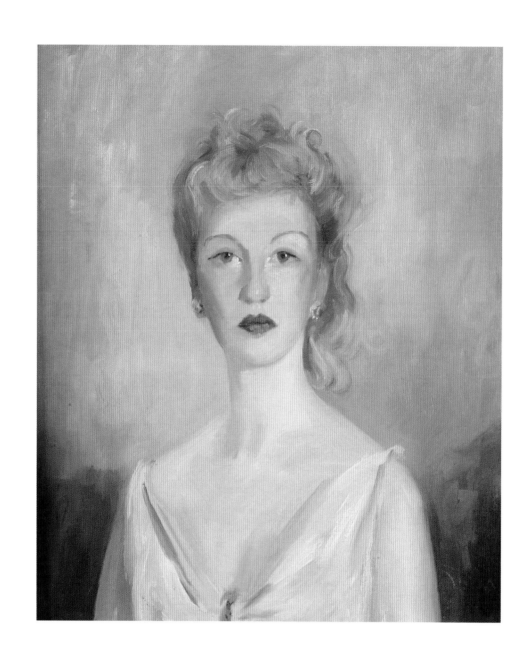

PHOEBE FOLGER

1947

PLATE 249

WARREN BUFFETT

1994

The Collection of Mr. Warren Buffett

PLATE 250

IRIS IN A COCOA POT

1996

PLATE 251

VIRGINIA CLINTON KELLEY

1993

The Collection of President William Jefferson Clinton

PLATE 252

AUDREY WITH TEA CUP

1 9 9 3

PLATE 253

IVA IN A NEW PARIS HAT

1938

PLATE 254

SELF PORTRAIT

1983

PLATE 255

THE SHEPHERD PHILOSOPHER
1992

PLATE 256

BLUE IRIS

1992

PLATE 257

PINK AND WHITE ZINNIAS
1996

PLATE 258

MAIN STREET, RIDGEFIELD

1987

PLATE 259

RED BARNS AND STORM CLOUDS
1974

PLATE 260

DAISIES IN A CRYSTAL VASE

1991

　　　　　PLATE 261

FRUIT BOWL
1984

PLATE 262   329

PROVINCETOWN CHURCH AND DOCK

1984

PLATE 263

BRIDGE AT STRATFORD
1990

PLATE 264   331

TRINITY CHURCH, SOUTHPORT
1990

PLATE 265

VISION OF HARTFORD

1990

The Collection of Governor Lowell P. Weicker, Jr.

PLATE 266

ARLES MAT AND APPLES
1970

PLATE 267

ARLES MAT AND APPLES II
1970

PLATE 268

PEACE ROSE

1980

PLATE 269

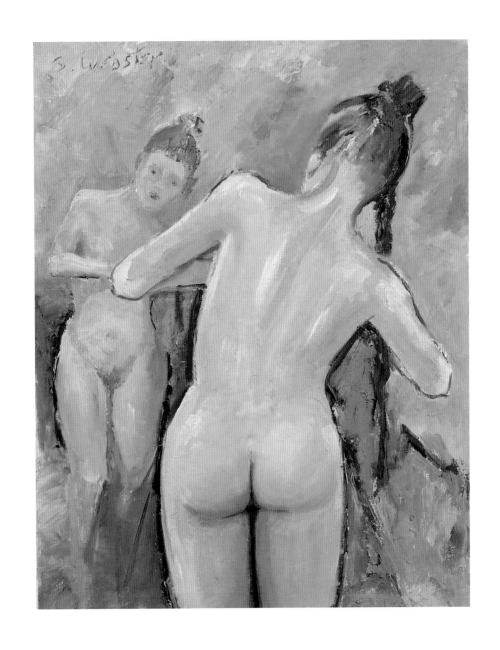

NUDE WITH REFELECTIONS
1983

PLATE 270

FLOWERS IN A COPPER VASE

1972

PLATE 271

BALCONY OVER THE SEA

1973

PLATE 272

STILL LIFE, KNIFE AND VEGETABLES
1971

PLATE 273

VEGETABLES AND WINE

1971

The Hickory Museum, North Carolina

PLATE 274

POPPIES IN A WHITE VASE

1972

PLATE 275

GEOMETRIC POPPIES

1963

The Collection of the Late Seymour Knox, Jr.

PLATE 276   343

STUDY IN BROWN, BLUE AND GREY

1978

Aslbright-Knox Gallery of Art, Buffalo, New York

344   PLATE 277

WHITE ROSE IN A BLUE VASE
1971

PLATE 278   345

RED WAGON ON BACK PORCH
1977

PLATE 279

BOWL OF FRUIT

1949

PLATE 280

347

BRIDGE IN THE PARK
1987

348   PLATE 281

THE YALE QUADRANGLE

1988

PLATE 282

PEONIES IN A PEWTER VASE

1971

PLATE 283

TWO DANCERS
1974

PLATE 284

AUDREY PAINTING
1994

PLATE 285

PAINTING AT ÉTRETAT

1992-1995

PAINTING IN THE LUXEMBOURG GARDENS

1977

PAINTING IN THE PARK AT ST. CLOUD

1995

SWD. 15.4 1938

VENICE, 1993

VENICE, 1938

S. Webster 74

FIVE SECOND SKETCHES FROM
IVA'S BALLET CLASS

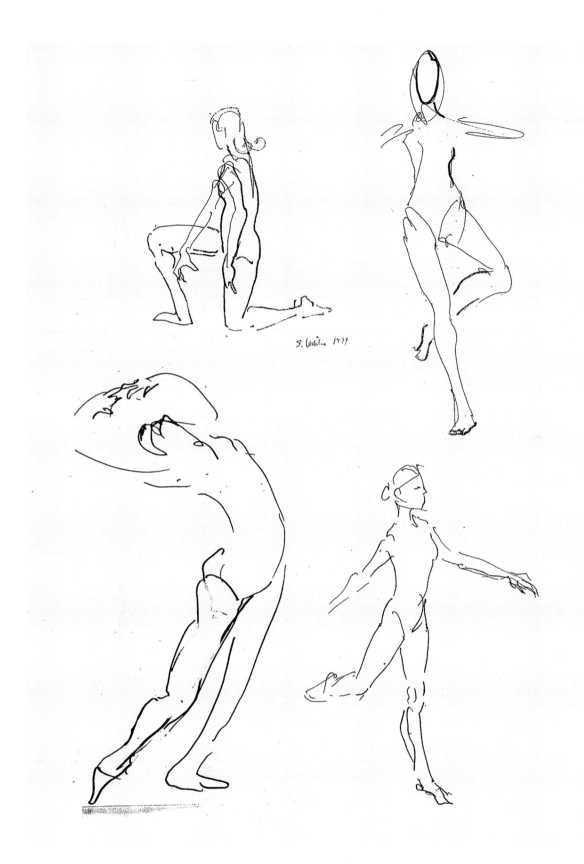

FIVE SECOND SKETCHES FROM
IVA'S BALLET CLASS

9

OLD MAN

1976

*Ink on paper—"American Drawings, 1976" Show 1975 American Drawings—
1976 Portsmouth Community Arts Center Portsmouth, Virginia.
Sole Juror, Felice Stampfle, Curator of drawings and prints, The Pierpoint Morgan Library, New York*

THE ORCHARD AT WEIR FARM
by Audrey Webster

TECHNIQUE

Lowery Sims asked me if I could tell her anything about my technique. I answered that I used such a multitude of techniques that there was no easy, short way to describe it. However, I said, I have some thoughts regarding technique in general that might be pertinent, and I can give you a thumbnail sketch of one of my procedures when painting out of doors.

First let me mention my thoughts about technique, as it applies to painting. It is of course an important element in making a good painting, but it is not, in my opinion, the most important. The most important ingredient, I believe, is the ability to "see the picture," to recognize what will make a good painting.

I have some of that and my wife Audrey has it too, to a surprising degree. I want to show you something that I think is remarkable, Audrey's paintings of "The Orchard at Weir Farm" and "The Bridge at Totnes." I think they illustrate my point about technique not being of paramount importance. At the time Audrey painted these, she had only been painting for two years and was eighty years old. No art school in the world would have you believe that you could acquire the technique in two years, to be able to paint these two pictures! Yet she painted them and without any help from me.

THE BRIDGE AT TOTNES

by Audrey Webster

I find them inspired paintings! I consider them, in some respects, superior to the two I painted of the same scenes at the same time. We usually set up our easels together, but not close enough to see each other's work. My two paintings are on page 260 (Pl 198) and page 366.

Look at the "Totnes" painting! Audrey has correctly recognized the brilliantly lit hill in the distance as the center point of the motif. I made the mistake of thinking that both the hill and its reflection in the river were the motif. The effect was to divide the point of interest and to weaken the picture. I think that you can see for yourself that she had a superior vision of each motif. I think that this ability to see is inborn. All I taught her was the basic bits of technique needed to mix colors and put them in the right place on the canvas!

Robert Henri wrote, "The artist should learn to gather for his work only the vital and express it with the keenest delight and emotion." The person who can sense the vital in what he sees, does not need to know all the various techniques that are taught in multi-year art school courses. What he does need is to find for himself a simple way to get what he sees transferred to the canvas. Some of the following suggestions might be helpful.

THE ORCHARD AT WEIR FARM
by S. Webster

COLOR

A good way to think of colors is as a German color manufacturer organized them years ago. Imagine them as a sphere, with the North Pole being white and the South Pole, black. The axis becomes the gray scale. Now place on the equator the brightest colors you can buy, arranged in the same order you observe in a rainbow, or the spectrum. Any color you can think of will have a proper place on some cord within this sphere. To have this organization in your head provides you with an instant clue to the quickest way to mix any color.

If you want to try mixing colors, it may be helpful to use a pallette and put out lots of white and relatively small amounts of the colors, always in the order of the spectrum. Now experiment with mixing each of the colors in turn with each other and with different amounts of white. You will, I believe, find this a fascinating occupation. Use a palette knife to do the mixing and have a box of facial tissues handy and a paper bag to throw the used tissue in. Wipe the knife clean between every mix and you will soon find that you can get any color you want.

D R A W I N G

To paint in the traditional style, it is necessary to be able to draw at least a little. Copying drawings by really good draftsmen, like Raphael or Degas, will teach you a lot. Not tracing! That will teach you nothing. You have to analyze their use of line, why it is heavy here and light there. How do they make the sweep of a line encompass volume and establish a third dimension? The five-second drawings of pupils in Iva's ballet class are not as easy to do as they may appear. You may think, "What of any thing great can one do in four or five seconds?". It is not the time it took to do the drawing that counts, it is the hours and hours that it took to learn the anatomy, the proportions and the laws of fore-shortening that allow you to concentrate on 'the gesture' which is unique to that moment. Both Degas and Rodin did many lightning fast sketches of the body in motion.

It is good to understand this, but it is not necessary to be expert at it, to paint "plein air" land-scapes. A basic understanding of linear perspective, however, is important.

When you go to paint outdoors, spend a lot of time finding a subject that truly inspires you. If you are not inspired, if you do not think it excitingly beautiful, there is not much chance that the painting you make will be beautiful.

Some easy tips! Use linen canvas or canvas panels. Stretched cotton sold in most stores is too flimsy. A French-type combination box and easel is a big help, especially in getting your wet painting back to the studio or hotel.

When you have your canvas set up, make a rough sketch of the motif very quickly with a small brush dipped in a dark paint like ultramarine thinned with turps. The quicker the better, for if you spend too much time at it, you are not going to want to wipe it out. The advantage of a quick sketch, wiped out and redone several times, is that each redo gives you a chance to improve the angle of vision and composition.

In order to arrive at a true set of values, cover almost all of the canvas (trying to save as much of the drawing as you can) with large areas of the approximate final tone values. The reason for this is that until most of the bright white canvas is covered, it is impossible to judge the correct value of details.

If you are properly engrossed in your subject, you will not even know if a crowd is watching you or not. You have a terrific job to complete in a very short time. It is short because you need to have the inspiration stay there to guide you, and with the sun and shadows moving, the effect after, say, three hours is going to be so different as to be confusing.

A painting done in one session like this is usually referred to as a sketch. That does not mean that it is necessarily inferior to a finished painting. If your observations in making this "sketch" have been keen and sensitive, the very fact that they were done quickly and without hesitation may make them more telling than a version of the subject done later from the sketch in the studio. The main reason for doing the picture again in the studio is not to try to make it better, just to make it larger. Paintings done "en plein air" have to be reasonably small because of the "sail" effect. You can easily be carried away, not by emotion, but by the breeze.

THE WASHINGTON POST and TIMES
HERALD
Sunday, March 3, 1952

Genius of Iva Kitchell
Shown in Dance Satire

By Paul Hume*

To give you some idea of Iva Kitchell I might say that she is something like Bea Lillie and Anna Russell rolled together. But that is fair to none of the three; each has her own genius. Only Miss K. seems to have enough genius for three.

Last night the Modern Dance Council proved itself both enterprising and incredibly foolish as it presented Iva Kitchell in a program of dance satire in Lisner Auditorium. Enterprising, because Iva Kitchell is one of the greatest entertainers alive today, and her entertainment rests solidly and constantly on a sure foundation of the techniques and attributes of many kinds of dance.

The project was foolish, at least for the Modern Dance Council, because anyone seeing Miss Kitchell do the routine called "Non Objective," which is the "Oh the Pain of It" branch of modern dance, will have more than a little difficulty ever taking modern dance seriously again.

There on the stage, Kitchell did, with hysteria-producing results among the audience, precisely the same things I am expected to review seriously when I go to a modern dance recital. There was the crotch-ripping, the pelvis snap, all of it laid bare by a woman whose body is her rapier, and whose mind must be one of the world's most amazing accumulations of genuine styles of song and dance from centuries past.

The great satirists of literature and the arts have been those whose knowledge of human weaknesses was the most penetrating. Miss Kitchell could stand with Swift for the brilliance of her spotlighting of the ridiculous elements in the dance today. Though the proper end of satire, to hope for some improvement in its subject, can hardly be in her mind as she works. She would be knifing her own livelihood if that happened.

No, the dance world will go on and we can be glad it will. But it will be a brighter place for Iva Kitchell, who does her whole show without leaving the stage, with comments, songs, patter, change of costumes and all, right before the delighted eyes of the audience. We hope she will hurry back, preferably next week. For the record, she takes off on the Zeigfield era, the operatic coloratura soprano, the fad for voodoo, and a hundred other things.

*Paul Hume, the Washington critic threatened with a fist fight by President Truman for having given his daughter, Margaret, a poor review on her singing debut.

THEATER ARTS

To Iva Kitchell, whose high-spirited New York audience almost filled the great reaches of Carnegie Hall, we are indebted for proof that dancing which is alleged to be funny, may be funny in actual fact. In the field of dance satire Miss Kitchell has no competitor. Unlike most dancers who try to poke fun at their colleagues, her technique is almost as secure as that of the artists whose foibles she exposes, whether she wears the classical tutu or the typical modern dancer's Mother Hubbard. With what sly malice she plays up the bad moments of classical ballet, as she freezes into a too solid arabesque, displays the prettiness of her hands and arms with self-satisfaction, or exaggerates the impression of elevation in an exit leap! And how knowingly she exposes the mock-profundity of some of the modern dances done to the accompaniment of recited words, as she stretches, turns, jumps scissorwise and falls groveling to the floor in order to interpret the aching text of Soul in Search!

HEAD OF IVA - TERRA COTTA

1 9 7 6

by Stokely Webster

S.W
FLAGSTAD. C-1940s

CARNEGIE HALL / Diamond Jubilee 75th Season

Friday Evening, November 4, 1966 at 8:30 o'clock

S. HUROK

presents

EUGENE ISTOMIN
Pianist

ISAAC STERN
Violinist

LEONARD ROSE
Cellist

PROGRAM

Trio in C Minor, Opus 1, No. 3	Beethoven

Allegro con brio
Andante cantabile con Variazioni
Menuetto: Quasi allegro
Finale: Prestissimo

Trio in B Major, Opus 8	Brahms

Allegro con brio
Scherzo — allegro molto
Adagio
Allegro

COLOR PLATE
INDEX

THE PLATES

Most of these paintings are in private collections

PARIS AND FRANCE

1   SAINT GERMAIN-EN-LAYE   1923
Oil on paper   8 x 11   KW 1

2   CHATEAU OF FRANCIS THE FIRST   1923
Conté on paper   8 x 11   KW 1
On back of Plate 1

3   CHAMPS ÉLYSÉES   1938
Oil on wood   13x16   KW 85
National Museum of American Art, Smithsonian Institution

4   PONT NEUF   1969
Oil on canvas   24x30   KW 352
The Collection of Audrey C. Webster

5   QUAI DU LOUVRE   1985
Oil on canvas   30x40   KW 664
The Collection of Mr. & Mrs Richard Kelly.

6   UNDER THE EIFFEL TOWER   1953
Oil on canvas   15x18   KW 208

7   PLACE FURSTENBERG   1990
Oil on canvas   18x24   KW 869

8   METRO LATOUR-MAUBOURG   1970
Oil on canvas   30x24   KW 361
The Museum of Fine Arts, St. Petersburg, Florida

9   SQUARE HENRI GALLI   1971
Oil on canvas   20x24   KW 377

10   LUXEMBOURG GARDENS   1960
Oil on canvas   18x24   KW 355
The Collection of Dr. Jane E. Ramsay

11   NOTRE DAME   1977
Oil on canvas   20x24   KW 514
The Collection of Audrey C. Webster

12   FACADE, NOTRE DAME   1994
Oil on canvas   22x28   KW 1106

13   NOTRE DAME   1993
Oil on canvas   16x20   KW 1088

14   TUILERIES POND   1979
Oil on canvas   14x18   KW 551
The Collection of Mrs. R. S. Webster

15   RAINY DAY IN PARIS   1984
Oil on canvas   20x24   KW 618
The Collection of Audrey C. Webster

16   NOTRE DAME DE PARIS   1996
Oil on canvas   30x24   KW 1217

17   PONT NEUF   1988
Oil on panel   14x18   KW 784

18   CHAMPS ÉLYSÉES   1995
Oil on canvas   24x30   KW 1191

19   PARK IN PARIS   1994
Oil on canvas   18x24   KW 1117

20   QUAI DE MONTEBELLO   1989
Oil on canvas   24x30   KW 817

21   ALLÉE THOMY THIERRY   1995
Oil on canvas   20x24   KW 1175
The Collection of Audrey C. Webster

22   PONT D'IÉNA   1995
Oil on canvas   20x24   KW 1165

23   SACRÉ COEUR   1989
Oil on canvas   20x24   KW 817
The Collection of Audrey C. Webster

24   MEDICI FOUNTAIN, LUXEMBOURG GARDENS   1992
Oil on canvas   22x28   KW 1002
The Collection of Audrey C. Webster

25   MEDICI FOUNTAIN, LUXEMBOURG GARDENS   1992
Oil on canvas   18x24   KW 872
Sold, Galerie Kornye, Dallas, Texas

26   NOTRE DAME IN STORM   1988
Oil on canvas   20x24   KW 794
The Collection of Mr. and Mrs. B. Doyle

27   THE SEINE, INSTITUT DES ARTS   1990
Oil on canvas   20x24   KW 865
The Collection of Audrey C. Webster

28   RUE ST. LAZARE   1988
Oil on canvas   24x20   KW 764
The Collection of Audrey C. Webster

29   PANTHÉON FROM ILE ST. LOUIS   1988
Oil on canvas   22x28   KW 763
The Collection of Audrey C. Webster

30   LUXEMBOURG GARDENS AND THE PANTHÉON   1987
Oil on canvas   22x28   KW 631

31   ALLÉE, LUXEMBOURG GARDENS   1985
Oil on canvas   24x30   KW 657
The Collection of Audrey C. Webster

32   LUXEMBOURG GARDENS, POND AND PANTHEON   1984
Oil on canvas   18x24   KW 622

33   LUXEMBOURG POND, FOUNTAIN   1988
Oil on canvas   24x30   KW 772
The Collection of Mr. & Mrs. Allport

34   PONT ROYAL AND THE LOUVRE   1989
Oil on canvas   20x24   KW 861

35   THE LOUVRE   1988
Oil on canvas   22x28   KW 796

36	AVENUE DES INVALIDES		1979
	Oil on canvas	24x30	KW 559
	The Collection of Audrey C. Webster		

37	BOULEVARD DE GRENELLE		1959
	Oil on canvas	24x20	KW 237
	The Collection of Audrey C. Webster		

38	QUAI DE LA CONFÉRENCE		1979
	Oil on canvas	14x18	KW 545

39	TUILLERIES POND		1979
	Oil on canvas	29x36	KW 552

40	VERSAILLE		1988
	Oil on canvas	22X28	KW 792

41	PARK, ST. CLOUD		1995
	Oil on panel	16x20	KW 1171

42	FOUNTAIN IN GRASSE		1990
	Oil on canvas	16x20	KW878
	The Collection of President & Mrs. Ronald Reagan		

43	PARK MONCEAU		1994
	Oil on canvas	22x28	KW 1105

44	AVENUE DE BRETEUIL		1998
	Oil on panel	14x18	KW 790
	Coll. Dr. and Mrs. Arthur D'Souza		

45	PLACE DUPLEIX		1979
	Oil on canvas	24x30	KW 541
	The Collection of Audrey C. Webster		

46	PARK IN POISSY		1994
	Oil on canvas	22x28	KW 1103

FRENCH COUNTRYSIDE

47	THE SEINE NEAR GIVERNY		1994
	Oil on canvas	18x24	KW 1115
	The Collection of Audrey C. Webster		

48	CASSIS		1953
	Oil on canvas	20x16	KW 211

49	ÉTRETAT		1992
	Oil on canvas	30x40	KW 1028

50	STORM AT ÉTRETAT		1992
	Oil on canvas	30x40	KW 1053

51	SAINT YON		1992
	Oil on panel	16x20	KW 1046
	Sold, IFI		

52	MORET		1992
	Oil on canvas	22x28	KW 1056

53	AVIGNON		1994
	Oil on canvas	16x20	KW 1113

54	VINEYARD OVER CASSIS		1987
	Oil on canvas	24x30	KW 703
	The Collection of Audrey C. Webster		

55	MORET SUR LOING		1995
	Oil on canvas	20x24	KW 1176

56	POPLARS ON THE ÉSSONE		1994
	Oil on canvas	28x22	KW 1129
	The Collection of Dr. & Mrs. Whitenech		

57	ORANGERY, STRASBOURG		1993
	Oil on panel	16x20	KW 1086

58	COURS MIRABEAU, AIX-EN-PROVENCE		1990
	Oil on canvas	22x28	KW 925
	The Collection of Audrey C. Webster		

59	ST. PIERRE, MONTFORD L'AMAURY		1991
	Oil on panel	16x20	KW 954
	The Collection of Audrey C. Webster		

60	PONT DU LOUP		1991
	Oil on canvas	20x24	KW 959

61	FARM IN THE ILE DE FRANCE		1994
	Oil on canvas	24x30	KW 1124

62	ROAD IN THE ILE DE FRANCE		1994
	Oil on canvas	22x28	KW 1114

63	CASTLE IN MANDELIEU		1992
	Oil on canvas	20x24	KW 1000

64	PLACE DE FORUM, ARLES		1992
	Oil on canvas	20x24	KW 999

65	SOISSY SUR ÉCOLE		1992
	Oil on panel	16x20	KW 1047

66	ALPHONSE DAUDET STATUE		1990
	Oil on panel	16x20	KW 884

67	THE SEINE AT HONFLEUR		1985
	Oil on canvas	24x30	KW 662
	The Collection of Dr. & Mrs. Robert Howell		

68	QUAI AT LA CIOTAT		1985
	Oil on canvas	24x30	KW 656
	The Collection of Dr. & Mrs. William Ramsay		

69	LA CIOTAT		1996
	Oil on canvas	22x28	KW 1201

70	CAFÉ DES ARTS, ST. TROPEZ		1991
	Oil on canvas	24x30	KW 988
	The Collection of Audrey C. Webster		

71	CHATEAU FONTCREUSE		1991
	Oil on canvas	22x28	KW 944

72	BESANCON		1994
	Oil on canvas	20x24	KW 1111

73	FORUM IN ARLES		1991
	Oil on canvas	20x24	KW 980
	The Collection of Mr. Graham Bond		

74	LILLA CABOT PERRY STUDIO		1992
	Oil on panel	16x20	KW 1049
	The Collection of Dr. & Mrs. William Ramsay		

75   PROMENADE AT GRASSE   1990
Oil on panel   16x20   KW 877
Sold IFI

76   PARK IN MENTON   1990
Oil on canvas   18x24   KW 873
The Collection of Audrey C. Webster

77   CAFÉ TERMINUS   1992
Oil on canvas   22x28   KW 998

78   STREET IN NIMES   1996
Oil on canvas   24x20   KW 1199

79   RAIN IN THE AUVERGNE   1974
Oil on canvas   22x28   KW 462
The Collection of Audrey C. Webster

80   STUDIO IN GOURDON   1992
Oil on panel   16x20   KW 1015
The Collection of General & Mrs. William Odom

81   CANAL IN STRASBOURG   1993
Oil on panel   16x20   KW 1085
The Collection of Dr. & Mrs. Terry Lenz

82   RIVER IN ANNECY   1992
Oil on canvas   24x30   KW 1035

83   MOULIN DE LA PLANCHE   1984
Oil on panel   16x20   KW 628
The Collection of Dr. and Mrs. William Ramsay

84   FOUNTAIN AT CASSIS   1969
Oil on canvas   18x24   KW 346

85   ORÁNGERIE, STRASBOURG   1994
Oil on canvas   22x28   KW 1104

86   JET D'EAU, ORÁNGERIE   1997
Oil on canvas   20x24   KW 1224

87   CARROUSEL IN NIMES   1991
Oil on canvas   22x28   KW 943

88   SEINE, PONT ALEXANDRE TROIS   1996
Oil on canvas   22x28   KW 1197
The Collection of Dr. and Mrs. William Ramsay

89   PONT ST. MICHEL   1974
Oil on canvas   24x30   KW 454
The Collection of Mrs. R. S. Webster

90   ÉGLISE FONTENAY MAUVOISIN   1992
Oil on panel   16x20   KW 1020
Sold Susan Conway Gallery, Washington, DC

91   COGNES SUR LOIRE   1971
Oil on canvas   24x30   KW 341

92   RAINBOW PASS NORTH OF PAMPLONA   1970
Oil on canvas   16x20   KW 370

93   RED BARNS NEAR ÉPINAL   1971
Oil on canvas   16x20   KW 384
The Collection of Frances Forbes

94   A ROAD IN FRANCE   1960
Oil on canvas   14x18   KW 264
The Collection of Elizabeth Howell

95   ST. ELIZABETH BRIDGE, BRUGGES   1989
Oil on canvas   22x28   KW 812
The Collection of David McCullough

96   PARK IN BRUGGES   1995
Oil on canvas   22x28   KW 1163

97   DOCK AT CHERBOURG   1971
Oil on canvas   24X20   KW 385

EARLY PAINTINGS

98   WILLOWS AND SKY   1929
Oil on canvas   19x23   KW 6

99   PROVINCETOWN BOAT   1930
Oil on canvas   9x12   KW 8

100   PROVINCETOWN TREE   1930
Oil on panel   20x16   KW 10

101   CHICAGO WATERTOWER   1933
Oil on panel   10x13   KW 19
The Collection of Mrs. R.S. Webster

102   COLUMBUS CIRCLE   1935
Oil on canvas   20x24   KW 44
The Collection of Audrey C. Webster

103   CHICAGO RAILYARD   1933
Oil on panel   10x13   KW 16
The Illinois State Museum, Springfield, Illinois

104   BROOKLYN BRIDGE   1936
Oil on canvas   20x24   KW 53
The Collection of Barbara Dyer

105   MADISON SQUARE   1950
Oil on canvas   20x24   KW 189
The Collection of Polk Public Museum, Lakeland, FL

106   HOUSE AT OREGON, ILLINOIS   1933
Oil on canvas   18x24   KW 39
The Collection of Audrey C. Webster

107   SELF PORTRAIT IN CAPE   1934
Oil on canvas   20x16   KW 43
The Collection of Audrey C. Webster

108   IVA WITH CAMEO   1937
Oil on canvas   20x16   KW 65
The Collection of Audrey C. Webster

109   IVA   1934
Oil on canvas   24x20   KW 42
The Collection of Audrey C. Webster

110   SELF PORTRAIT   1934
Oil on panel   18x14   KW 41
The Collection of Audrey C. Webster

111   IVA LOOKING OVER SHOULDER   1951
Oil on canvas   24x18   KW 200
The Collection of Audrey C. Webster

112   IVA IN WHITE FRILL BLOUSE   1937
Oil on canvas   20x16   KW64

113 CENTRAL PARK AT SEVENTH AVENUE   1939
Oil on canvas   11x13   KW 90.2

114 CENTRAL PARK, WEST DRIVE   1937
Oil on canvas   18x24   KW 77
The Collection of Ronald Pisano

115 I VA WITH WINE GLASS   1938
Oil on canvas   46x32   KW 94

116 MARIA THERESA ACUNA   1950
Oil on canvas   46x32   KW 185
The Collection of Audrey C. Webster

117 HUGH NORTON   1938
Oil on canvas   20x16   KW 79

118 HELEN DERMOLINSKA   1950
Oil on canvas   28x22   KW 173

119 LITTLE NECK BAY   1945
Oil on canvas   20x24   KW 136

120 FRUIT BOWL   1949
Oil on canvas   18x24   KW 153

121 UNIVERSITY CLUB   1940
Oil on canvas   20x24   KW 105
Daytona Museum of Art, Florida

122 TIMES SQUARE, SUNDAY MORNING   1940
Oil on canvas   24x20
Museum of The City Of New York

123 SELF PORTRAIT WITH PIPE   1937
Oil on canvas   30x24   KW 61
Denver Museum Of Art, Colorado

124 JOSSEY WITH WINE GLASS   1937
Oil on canvas   24x20   KW 697

125 BETS ON BEACH   1945
Oil on canvas   20x16   KW 167
The Collection of Elizabeth Howell

126 BETS   1950
Oil on canvas   24x18   KW 198
The Collection of Audrey C. Webster

127 IVA IN BEFORE THE BALL   1949
Oil on canvas   24x20   KW 162

128 MODEL RESTING   1949
Oil on panel   14x18   KW 149
The Phillips Collection, Washington, DC

129 STORM ON SOUTH SHORE   1944
Oil on canvas   18x24   KW 127

130 CENTRAL PARK SOUTH   1943
Oil on canvas   20x24   KW 124
Cornell Art Center, Winter Park, Florida

131 PEGGY KORN   1950
Oil on canvas   30x24   KW 186
The Collection of Peggy Harriman Korn

132 IVA IN BLACK VELVET DRESS   1938
Oil on canvas   24x18   KW 89
The High Museum of Art, Atlanta, Georgia

133 KEY WEST STREET   1949
Oil on canvas   18x24   KW 151
The Collection of Harry Rand

134 HAVANA HARBOR   1949
Oil on canvas   20x24   KW 159
The Daytona Museum of Art, Florida

135 IVA IN STRAW HAT   1950
Oil on canvas   20x16   KW 196
The Collection of Audrey C. Webster

136 IVA   1945
Oil on panel   24x20   KW 129

137 JONES BEACH   1948
Oil on canvas   20x24   KW 145
The Collection of Dr. Gary Libby

138 THE BEACH   1945
Oil on canvas   20x24   KW 130
The Indianapolis Museum of Art, Indiana

139 IVA AND HARVEY,
23RD STREET STUDIO   1951
Oil on panel   2x15   KW 201

140 MADISON SQUARE PARK   1949
Oil on canvas   22x28   KW 156
The Frye Museum, Seattle, Washington

141 CUT GLASS   1949
Oil on panel   16x12   KW 164
The Collection of Mr. & Mrs. Duncan Healy

142 IVA IN FLOWER HAT   1945
Oil on canvas   18x14   KW 138
The Indianapolis Museum of Art, Indiana

143 IVA AS CHORUS GIRL   1945
Oil on canvas   24x20   KW128
The Parrish Museum, Southampton, New York

144 THE SEA CAPTAIN   1950
Oil on canvas   36x24   KW 178

145 MARY HUTCHINSON   1936
Oil on canvas   16x12   KW 55

146 KIRSTEN OLSEN   1950
Oil on canvas   30x24   KW 182

147 FIFTH AVENUE AT CENTRAL PARK   1936
Oil on canvas   20x24   KW 49

148 THREE LIMP ROSES   1967
Oil on canvas   24x18   KW 322
The Collection of Audrey C. Webster

149 AFRICAN VIOLETS   1968
Oil on canvas   16x13   KW 328

150 PORT WASHINGTON   1941
Oil on canvas   20x24   KW121

151 CARROUSEL   1940
Oil on canvas   18x24   KW 104

152 CARRIAGE IN THE PARK   1938
Oil on canvas   11x13   KW 90.1
The Collection of Audrey C. Webster

153 IVA ON BALCONY   1953
    Oil on canvas   14x11   KW 214
    The Collection of Mrs. R. S. Webster

154 IVA IN WHITE LEOTARD   1959
    Oil on canvas   24x20   KW 251

155 STEPHIE   1953
    Oil on canvas   18x15   KW 215

156 THE BLUE TIGHTS   1961
    Oil on canvas   28x22   KW 267

157 COMPOTE WITH FRUIT   1966
    Oil on canvas   20x16   KW 315
    The Collection of Ronald Pisano

158 STILL LIFE WITH DECORATED VASE   1971
    Oil on canvas   20x16   KW 380

159 FRENCH BREAD AND BOTTLE   1965
    Oil on canvas   20x24   KW 296
    The Collection of Audrey C. Webster

160 CARAFE ON TRAY   1967
    Oil on canvas   18x24   KW 323
    The Collection of Dr. & Mrs. Robert Howell

N E W   Y O R K

161 NIAGARA FALLS   1992
    Oil on canvas panel   22x28   KW 726
    Albright-Knox Gallery of Art, Buffalo, New York

162 FIFTH AVENUE SOUTH OF
    METROPOLITAN   1987
    Oil on canvas   24x30   KW 696

163 FIFTH AVENUE THE METROPOLITAN   1987
    Oil on canvas   24x30   KW 1157
    The Collection of Audrey C. Webster

164 THE POND AT CENTRAL PARK   1985
    Oil on canvas   24x30   KW 1112

165 THE PLAZA FOUNTAIN   1985
    Oil on canvas   24x30   KW 650

166 FIFTH AVENUE AT 60TH STREET   1988
    Oil on canvas   18x24   KW 767

167 THE SAILBOAT POND   1983
    Oil on canvas   24x30   KW 585
    The Collection of Audrey C. Webster

168 FIFTH AVENUE BY THE PARK   1983
    Oil on canvas   24x30   KW580

169 THE GUGGENHEIM MUSEUM   1987
    Oil on canvas   24x30   KW 692

170 CENTRAL PARK AT SEVENTH AVENUE   1985
    Oil on canvas   24x30   KW 655

171 THE POND, CENTRAL PARK   1988
    Oil on canvas   20x24   KW 791
    Sold, Chapellier Gallery, NY 1986

172 THE PLAZA FROM 61ST STREET   1987
    Oil on canvas   22x28   KW 689

173 THE PLAZA FROM 60TH STREET   1987
    Oil on canvas   22x28   KW 693
    The Collection of Audrey C. Webster

174 FIFTH AVENUE, LOOKING NORTH   1985
    Oil on canvas   24x30   KW 651
    The Collection of Norman J. Coutant Jr.

175 ENTRANCE TO THE PARK   1985
    Oil on canvas   24x30   KW 652
    Sold by Chapellier Gallery 1987

176 BROADWAY AT COLUMBUS AVENUE   1983
    Oil on canvas   22x28   KW 584
    The Collection of Harold C. Schonberg

177 THE POND, LOOKING EAST   1987
    Oil on canvas   22x28   KW 690
    The Collection of Dr. & Mrs. Robert Howell

178 BROOKLYN BRIDGE   1983
    Oil on canvas   22x28   KW 583
    The Collection of Austin Kiplinger

179 FIFTH AVENUE, THE GUGGENHEIM   1987
    Oil on canvas   30x40   KW 691

180 WILSON HARBOR   1986
    Oil on canvas   22x28   KW 679
    The Collection of Mr. & Mrs. Norman J. Coutant Jr.

181 SANDY HARBOR   1987
    Oil on canvas   18x24   KW 781
    The Collection of Mr. & Mrs. Norman J. Coutant Jr.

182 FIFTH AVENUE WITH CARRIAGE   1987
    Oil on canvas   24X30   KW 694
    The Collection of Audrey C. Webster

L O N D O N ,   E N G L A N D

183 HOUSES OF PARLIAMENT   1996
    Oil on canvas   30x24   KW 1218

184 WESTMINSTER BRIDGE   1992
    Oil on canvas   24x30   KW 1043
    The Collection of Mr. & Mrs. Richard Kelly

185 HOUSES OF PARLIAMENT   1992
    Oil on canvas   24x30   KW 1030

186 WESTMINSTER BRIDGE   1989
    Oil on canvas   20x24   KW 840

187 TOWER BRIDGE   1996
    Oil on canvas   30x24   KW 1221

188 FARM IN BEDFORDSHIRE   1989
    Oil on canvas   18x24   KW 848

189 RIVER AT CAMBRIDGE   1989
    Oil on canvas   20x24   KW 644
    The Collection of Mr. & Mrs. Richard Kelly

190	BATH ON AVON		1989
	Oil on canvas	20x24	KW 854
	The Collection of Mr. & Mrs Donald Parker		

191	BRIDGES ON THE CAM RIVER		1989
	Oil on canvas	20x24	KW 851
	The Collection of Mr. and Mrs. C. Edwards		

192	BRIDGE IN CAMBRIDGE		1994
	Oil on canvas	22x28	KW 1149
	The Collection of Mr. & Mrs. B. Shreve		

193	BRIDGE OF SIGHS		1989
	Oil on canvas	20x24	KW 843
	The Collection of Audrey C. Webster		

194	PUNTS ON THE CAM RIVER		1989
	Oil on canvas	20x24	KW 856
	The Collection of Audrey C. Webster		

195	BRIDGE ON THE CAM RIVER		1989
	Oil on canvas	20x24	KW 842
	The Collection of Dr. & Mrs. Terry Lenz		

196	WATERMILL IN WALES		1989
	Oil on canvas	20x24	KW 849
	The Collection of Mr. & Mrs. Jonathan Webster		

197	SERPENTINE AT HYDE PARK		1989
	Oil on panel	16x20	KW 834
	The Collection of Mr. & Mrs. Roy Lenz		

198	BRIDGE AT TOTNES 1995		
	Oil on panel	16x20	KW 1173
	Sold IFI		

VENICE

199	PIAZZA S. MARCO		1993
	Oil on canvas	30x40	KW 1061

200	THREE PALACES ON THE GRAND CANAL		1990
	Oil on canvas	22x28	KW 923

201	SANTA MARIA DELLA SALUTE		1992
	Oil on canvas	30x24	KW 1220

202	PUNTA DELLA DOGANA		1992
	Oil on canvas	30x40	KW 1042

203	DOGES PALACE		1996
	Oil on canvas	30x24	KW 1219

204	PALACES ON THE GRAND CANAL		1990
	Oil on canvas	20x24	KW 922

205	PIAZETTA S. MARCO		1992
	Oil on canvas	24x30	KW 1039
	The Collection of Mr. & Mrs. Robert Nolan		

206	GONDOLA ON A SIDE CANAL		1991
	Oil on canvas	24x20	KW 942
	The Collection of Ms. Leigh Firestone		

207	LOGGIA IN VENICE		1991
	Oil on canvas	22x28	KW 971
	The Collection of Mr. & Mrs. Richard Kelly		

208	GRAND CANAL, VENICE		1990
	Oil on canvas	20x24	KW 870

209	CHIESA DELLA SALUTE		1990
	Oil on canvas	22x28	KW 929

210	LA SALUTE		1994
	Oil on canvas	26x40	KW 1161

211	VENICE, BRIDGE OF SIGHS		1994
	Oil on canvas	24x18	KW 1154

212	C' DA MOSTA		1991
	Oil on canvas	20x24	KW 928

213	PALACE IN VENICE		1990
	Oil on canvas	16x20	KW 889
	The Collection of Mr. & Mrs. Marshall Tillman		

214	THE RIALTO BRIDGE		1992
	Oil on canvas	24x30	KW 1038

215	THE RIALTO BRIDGE, VENICE		1990
	Oil on canvas	20x24	KW 892

216	S. GIORGIO MAGGIORE		1990
	Oil on panel	16x20	KW 881

217	CAMPONILE AND DOGES PALACE		1990
	Oil on canvas	20x24	KW 888
	The Collection of Dr. & Mrs. Robert Howell		

218	S. GIORGIO MAGGIORE AT DUSK		1996
	Oil on canvas	22x28	KW 1214

219	ENTRANCE TO THE GRAND CANAL		1996
	Oil on canvas	24x30	KW 1216

220	BACINO S. MARCO		1996
	Oil on canvas	24x30	KW 1213

221	STORM IN VENICE		1992
	Oil on canvas	30x40	KW 992

THE SEA

222	BEACH AT DEAUVILLE		1975
	Oil on canvas	16x13	KW 478
	The Collection of Jafar Falasiri		

223	FIRE ISLAND BEACH		1980
	Oil on canvas	16x20	KW 564

224	THE FIRE ISLAND BEACH		1994
	Oil on canvas	24x30	KW 1146

225	THE BEACH AT ORMOND		1984
	Oil on canvas	20x24	KW 602
	The Collection of Dr. Jane E. Ramsay		

226	HALIFAX RIVER, SEA BREEZE PARK		1984
	Oil on canvas	22x28	KW 646
	The Collection of Mrs. R. S.Webster		

227	THE BEACH AT ORMOND BY THE SEA		1985
	Oil on canvas	20x24	KW 668
	Sold Chapellier Gallery 1988		

| 228 | SAILBOATS ON BEACH IN FOG | | 1978 |

228 SAILBOATS ON BEACH IN FOG   1978
     Oil on canvas   18x24   KW527
     The Collection of Mr. & Mrs. Anders M. Johnson

229 BEACH AT SUNSET   1976
     Oil on canvas   13x18   KW 499
     The Collection of Mr. & Mrs. Roy Lenz

230 SASCO BEACH   1985
     Oil on canvas   20x24   KW 670

231 ROCKS AT WASHINGTON OAKS   1983
     Oil on canvas   18x24   KW 597
     The Collection of Audrey C. Webster

232 THE GULFSTREAM AT
     WASHINGTON OAKS   1995
     Oil on canvas   26x40   KW 1162

233 SPANISH BEACH   1988
     Oil on canvas   20x24   KW 777
     The Collection of Jon Monson

234 BOATS AT NOANK   19
     Oil on canvas   22x28   KW 1185
     Sold, Galerie Kornye 98

235 SAUGATUCK SHORES   1995
     Oil on canvas   20x24   KW 1187
     Sold, IFI

236 WEST CHOP, MARTHAS VINEYARD   1989
     Oil on panel   14x18   KW 827

237 RIVERSIDE AT NOANK   1986
     Oil on canvas   20x24   KW 742
     The Collection of Mr. & Mrs. Vincent Costanzo

238 STRATFORD BRIDGE   1987
     Oil on canvas   22x28   KW 744

239 BEACH AT MADISON   1987
     Oil on canvas   9x12   KW 731
     The Collection of Ms. Caitlin Kelly

240 SHINNECOCK INLET   1976
     Oil on canvas   16x20   KW 495

241 THE WAVE   1984
     Oil on canvas   20x24   KW 604

242 ROUGH SEA   1988
     Oil on canvas   14x18   KW 773

243 THE ROAD AT DUSK   1984
     Oil on canvas   16x20   KW 605
     The Collection of Mr. and Mrs. Julian Gregory

PORTRAITS AND STIL-LIFES

244 YELLOW MUMS   1992
     Oil on canvas panel 20x16   KW 1052

245 MUGUET ET RHODODENDRON   1991
     Oil on canvas   20x16   KW 956

246 PINK ROSES   1992
     Oil on canvas   20x16   KW 1025

247 SANDRA   1974
     Oil on canvas   24x18   KW 440
     The Collection of Mr. & Mrs. Richard Kelly

248 AUDREY   1986
     Oil on canvas   20x16   KW 685
     The Collection of Audrey C. Webster

249 PHOEBE FOLGER   1947
     Oil on canvas   24x20   KW 143

250 WARREN BUFFET   1994
     Oil on canvas   24x20   KW 1122
     The Collection of Mr. Warren Buffett

251 IRIS IN A COCOA POT   1996
     Oil on canvas   24x20   KW 1203

252 VIRGINIA CLINTON KELLEY   1993
     Oil on canvas   24x18   KW 1090
     The Collection of President William Jefferson Clinton

253 AUDREY WITH TEACUP   1993
     Oil on canvas   24x20   KW 1065
     The Collection of Audrey C. Webster

254 IVA IN A NEW PARIS HAT   1938
     Oil on canvas   20x16   KW 88

255 SELF PORTRAIT   1983
     Oil on canvas   20x16   KW 574
     The Collection of Audrey C. Webster

256 THE SHEPHERD PHILOSOPHER   1992
     Oil on canvas   20x16   KW 1055
     The Collection of Audrey C. Webster

257 BLUE IRIS   1992
     Oil on canvas   24x20   KW 1001
     The Collection of Dr. J Webb

258 PINK AND WHITE ZINNIAS   1996
     Oil on canvas   20x16   KW 1211

259 MAIN STREET, RIDGEFIELD   1987
     Oil on canvas   22x28   KW 737
     The Collection of Mr. & Mrs. Roy Lenz

260 RED BARNS AND STORM CLOUDS   1974
     Oil on canvas   30x24   KW 452

261 DAISIES IN A CRYSTAL VASE   1991
     Oil on canvas   20x16   KW 94

262 FRUIT BOWL   1984
     Oil on canvas   16x20   KW 610
     The Collection of Mr. & Mrs. William Ramsay

263 PROVINCETOWN CHURCH AND DOCK   1984
     Oil on canvas   18x24   KW 598
     The Collection of Stephanie Brooks

264 BRIDGE AT STRATFORD   1990
     Oil on canvas   24x30   KW 914
     The Collection of Dr. & Mrs. Robert Howell

265	TRINITY CHURCH, SOUTHPORT		1990
	Oil on canvas	22x28	KW 899
	The Collection of Dr. and Mrs. Terry Lenz		

266	VISION OF HARTFORD		1990
	Oil on canvas	30x40	KW 913
	The Collection of Mr. Lowell P. Weicker, Jr.		

267	ARLES MATS AND APPLES		1970
	Oil on canvas	18x24	KW 358

268	ARLES MATS AND APPLES II		1970
	Oil on canvas	18x24	KW 359

269	PEACE ROSE		1980
	Oil on canvas	30x24	KW 562
	The Collection of Dr.& Mrs.Robert Howell		

270	NUDE WITH REFLECTIONS		1983
	Oil on canvas	24x20	KW 575
	The Collection of Dr. Mario Salin		

271	FLOWERS IN A COPPER VASE		1972
	Oil on canvas	24x18	KW 405

272	BALCONY OVER THE SEA		1973
	Oil on canvas	24x30	KW 437
	The Collection of Susan & Paul Hammaker		

273	STILL LIFE, KNIFE AND VEGETABLES		1971
	Oil on canvas	22x28	KW 373
	The Collection of Mr. & Mrs. Richard Kelly		

274	VEGETABLES AND WINE		1971
	Oil on canvas	22x28	KW 378

275	POPPIES IN A WHITE VASE		1972
	Oil on canvas	24x30	KW 412

276	GEOMETRIC POPPIES		1963
	Oil on canvas	24x20	KW 290
	The Collection of The late Seymour Knox, Jr.		

277	STUDY IN BROWN BLUE AND GRAY		1978
	Oil on canvas	30x40	KW 525
	Albright-Knox Art Gallery, Buffalo, New York		

278	WHITE ROSE IN A BLUE VASE		1971
	Oil on canvas	24x20	KW 398

279	RED WAGON ON BACK PORCH		1977
	Oil on canvas	30x40	KW 523
	The Collection of Mr. & Mrs. Richard Kelly		

280	BOWL OF FRUIT		1945
	Oil on canvas	18x24	KW 152

281	BRIDGE IN THE PARK		1987
	Oil on canvas	22x28	KW 698

282	THE YALE QUADRANGLE		1988
	Oil on canvas	18x24	KW 779

283	PEONIES IN A PEWTER VASE		1971
	Oil on canvas	24x20	KW 396

284	TWO DANCERS		1974
	Oil on canvas	30x24	KW 444
	The Collection of Mr. & Mrs. Mark Webre		

285	AUDREY, PAINTING		1994
	Oil on canvas	20x24	KW 1141
	The Collection of Mr. and Mrs Jean Boulle		